The Beginning Writer's Handbook

Edited By

Kirk Polking and Jean Chimsky

Writer's Digest—Funk & Wagnalls
380 Madison Avenue, New York, New York 10017

Preface

The letters in this book reflect the questions writers most often ask the editors of *Writer's Digest*. The questions are grouped under 38 subject categories.

In the case of questions on actual contracts and other business matters, writers are advised to consult an attorney. We can only offer information about the practical experiences of writers, not specific legal advice.

If you would like to refer to a previous issue of *Writer's Digest* mentioned in these pages, please consult back copies in your public library, since unfortunately we have no back issues available for sale. Many libraries, in addition to their subscription copies, now also have *Writer's Digest* on microfilm. Beginning with the January, 1968 issue, *Writer's Digest* is now indexed in the *Reader's Guide to Periodical Literature*.

The detailed cross-index by subject on page 161 may help you turn up answers to some questions you don't find under the expected chapter heading.

If a question that's been bothering *you* lately doesn't appear in this book, write the editors so that other freelancers may benefit in the next edition of this book.

Contents

Chapter 1

How To Find Addresses

Writing the "Name" Author

Q. I am anxious to write Graham Greene a letter. How might I get in touch with him?

A. Graham Greene could be contacted by sending him a letter in care of his publisher, Viking Press, 625 Madison Avenue, New York, N.Y. 10022.

Forwarding Address

Q. I wish to write a letter to England's former Poet Laureate, John Masefield. Please let me know how I may get in touch with him.

A. Mr. Masefield is deceased but his publisher is The MacMillan Company, 866 Third Avenue, New York, N.Y. 10022.

Writing The Voice

Q. Could you tell me where I might address a letter to Frank Sinatra, with the prevailing odds concerning his chance of getting to read it.

A. I'm no expert on the address at which Mr. Sinatra most conscientiously reads his mail, but you might try writing to him in care of Reprise Records, 1347 Cahuenga Boulevard, Hollywood, California.

Authors' Addresses

Q. Where can I get the addresses of authors? For example: Ray Bradbury, James Baldwin, Philip Wylie, etc.?

A. Write to the novelists in care of their publishers and to the short story writers in care of the magazines in which their stories appeared.

How Reach Disney?

Q. Can you furnish the name of the agency I must go through to reach Walt Disney Producers?

A. Please see the list of accredited Authors' Agents handling original TV and movie scripts in the latest edition of *Writer's Market*.

Chapter 2

What About Literary Agents?

Two Agents?

Q. Can you tell me whether or not it is ethical to have two agents? In this case one in Los Angeles, and one in New York. Each handles the same type of material, but in his own locale. Do agents frown on this procedure even though the material submitted to each is not the same?

A. It is more ethical to have only one agent handling all your material of the same type. Confidence in your agent should not be limited by geographical boundaries. If one specialized in books and the other in TV scripts, that would be another matter.

Agency Problem

Q. I paid a literary agency for criticism-analysis of two children's stories. They notified me of the opinions of various publishers; but when I asked to whom they showed these stories, they didn't answer my letter. Did I have a right to ask the names of the publishers?

A. You did indeed. Any reputable agency would not hesitate to reveal the publishers to whom they had submitted material.

One Agent At A Time

Q. If a book or story is in the hands of an agent, is it possible to make such arrangements that a copy may be submitted to another agent or to a publisher while it is still in the hands of the first agent?

A. Once a manuscript has been turned over to one agent, it is not ethical to submit copies either to another agent or to a publisher. If you feel the agent is not handling your work to your satisfaction, ask for its return and you shall then be free to try marketing it yourself or to place it with another agent.

Return of Ms

Q. Where an agency ignores a request to return a book manuscript, other than continuing to write letters, what recourse does a writer have? Is there some organization set up for the protection of writers to whom they might appeal?

A. The best procedure is to write a registered letter to the agency stating that you are withdrawing the manuscript from their consideration and resubmitting it elsewhere. It means you'll have to retype it, but it will save you much more in time and frustration. *Writer's Digest* would like to be notified whenever you have difficulty getting either payment or reports on your manuscripts, so we can check this information with other complaints in our file and consider publishing a notice in our "Storm Warnings" department of the Mailbag.

Handle on Speculation?

Q. I have a lot of manuscripts but all need to be revised. But I'm on a pension and haven't money to pay for the work. Is there anyone who will revise and sell, take out their share of the money and send me the rest?

A. No agent is willing or financially able to do revision work on speculation, in the hope that he will be paid eventually out of the sale of the work. Perhaps eventually, by studying *Writer's Digest* and the magazines to which you would like to submit, you would be able to learn to revise your own manuscripts and resubmit them for sale. Good luck!

Agency Requirements?

Q. Can you tell me what the requirements are for becoming a literary agent or tell me where I may obtain such information?

A. The requirements for becoming a literary agent are those of knowing the publishing market so well that you can prove to prospective clients that you are able to successfully place the work of professional writers with magazine and book editors. Many literary agents came to their jobs after successfully marketing their own work or through being editors in the field and knowing what publishers want to buy.

Agents for Puzzles?

Q. Are there—and if so, who are they —agencies that handle crosswords, crostics and double crostics?

A. Most agents are interested only in handling authors who do books, television scripts, and other more profitable-length manuscripts. The financial return on items such as crosswords, filler material, poetry, etc. is so small, no agencies can afford to handle just those. There are, of course, a great many magazines which use crossword puzzles other than crossword puzzle magazines themselves. They are listed throughout our annual directory, *The Writer's Market*.

Recommended List?

Q. How will I know whether an agent is reputable or not? Is there a printed list I can obtain of recommended agents? I am uncertain as to the qualifications of the company who is representing my interests and I would like to check on its qualifications. The comparative group I have in mind is the Better Business for companies. Would they also handle Literary Agents?

A. Yes, a Better Business Bureau in the city in which your prospective literary agent is located, could let you know whether or not they have had any complaints about their business operation. The other way you could check on the reputation of the agent is to ask him to give you the names and addresses of three of his clients whom you could write for information about his work with them.

Agents for Illustrators?

Q. Could you provide me with the names and addresses of agents who represent illustrators, artists, and photographers?

A. The Manhattan Yellow Pages lists artists' agents and photographers' agencies. No doubt your local public library has a copy of the Manhattan Yellow Pages you could consult.

Chapter 3

Article Problems

Resubmit?

Q. I have written some articles that I would like to see in more than one magazine. When I write for religious papers, I do not ask for any pay for the articles. But I take several of these magazines myself and would like to send the articles to each one. Would this be legal? If these were paid for, would it be legal then to send to another editor?

A. For these unpaid articles, it would be best to write a query letter to the other publications, informing them of your generous offer and indicating where these articles originally appeared. Prior to doing this, however, it would be safe to check with the publication that first printed the material to see whether it would have any objection to reprints in other magazines. This same procedure of checking with the publications involved would apply in the case of payment for the articles. But here you would have to ascertain whether or not you sold the reprint rights.

Anecdotes

Q. I need advice about use of anecdotes in articles: do they have to be exactly from life to be ethical; how about making one up to suit the need?

A. If you're going to mention the names of actual people, then you'd better stick to real-life facts. But if you want to make up an anecdote to illustrate a point in a nonfiction article, then you might preface it with something like: "It's the sort of town where something like the following could easily happen:—" . . . or "There's a rumor going around that—" . . . or "I wouldn't be surprised if—." You see, in this way the point can be made, but without giving the erroneous idea that the incident actually did take place. The secret of good anecdote-telling is the ability to spot a small true-life happening and describe it in such a way that your interpretation gives it new dimension and significance.

Recipe Sales

Q. During a spring trip to the Pacific

Northwest, I developed a form of "oven" camp cooking along with some special recipes. One recipe involves the use of six nationally known food products. I wish to achieve two objectives: 1) the presentation of the six-product recipe to the individual companies involved; 2) an illustrated article describing the "oven" cooking including all the recipes. How might I offer the recipes six separate times to the six companies? Could I then, if any one of them used the recipe, retain the rights to incorporate this six-product recipe in the article to be presented early next year to a magazine devoted to outdoor living and camping?

A. You might be putting the dessert before the main dish here. You would do better *first* to write the article featuring the recipe. If and when it appears in that camping magazine, you could then send six copies of this published article to the six companies. These companies will no doubt be pleased to learn of this original use of their product, but do not expect any remuneration from them for this.

Chapter 4

Writing and Selling Books

Query a Book Publisher?

Q. Is it permissible to write a book company regarding the status of a novel? I sent out a manuscript a month ago, and so far have heard nothing. Also, would you explain in your column about sample chapters and outlines?

A. It's permissible, but you're too impatient. It sometimes takes over three months for a publisher to report on a book-length manuscript. You'd get faster service on an outline, two or three sample chapters and a short cover letter asking if the publisher is interested in seeing more. The outline should be brief, about a page or two, depending on how long it takes to summarize the main incidents of the story.

Book Illustrator

Q. I have a manuscript for a children's book, a fantasy, but need someone to illustrate it. It would be on a 50/50 basis and quite a few line drawings would be needed. How would you suggest I contact that sort of person?

A. Concentrate on selling your story to a book publisher and then let *him* worry about the illustrations. He prefers to do this anyway, since he is familiar with the various styles and abilities of different illustrators, and can select the one whose talents would be most appropriate for your subject matter and for the format he wishes to use.

Publishing Your Own Book

Q. If I have a book published or I print it on my own with a mimeo machine and I have it copyrighted and I advertise and sell a few copies of it, will I at any time be able to offer this same book to a larger publisher, or do you think this would ruin my chances of selling it to a larger firm?

A. Before printing this book on your own, first see if any "larger publisher" would be interested in it. Private printing and sale of copies would usually lessen established publishers' interest in a work since they would prefer to be the first to present and distribute the manuscript in book form.

Nonfiction Book

Q. I have a nonfiction book on the order of a self-help psychology type. It is written like a test in order to pique the reader's mind; also it is in regular manuscript form in some places. I would like to know whether I should send it to a publisher straight off or after a query or through an agent? As I am 21 and this is my first book, should I get it notarized? Should a manuscript be sent by registered mail? Could you suggest some suitable publishers?

A. Query the publisher first and then if he expresses interest, you can submit the completed manuscript. In your letter, you might include excerpts from one of the tests and from the standard prose passages, too, so that the publisher can get an idea of your style and treatment. Notarization is not necessary since unpublished manuscripts are protected by common law copyright. If you keep a carbon copy of your manuscript, you don't really need to send it out by costly registered mail. Consult *Writer's Market* for the names and addresses of book publishers who would be interested in your subject matter.

Book Award

Q. Could you give me any information on the Newberry and Caldecott Awards? How do you get a book nominated?

A. These awards are given annually through the American Library Association by a member committee of children's and school librarians. Usually in November, members of the Children's Library Association receive blanks for nominating their choices for the Awards. For further details about these Awards, please see *A History of the Newberry and Caldecott Medals* by Irene Smith (Viking Press, New York, 1957).

Book Synopsis and Outline

Q. Should a synopsis be overall or abbreviated chapter by chapter content? How extensive should an outline be?

A. A synopsis should provide a comprehensive summary of the contents in about two typewritten pages. An outline could cover chapter by chapter highlights.

Chapters and Synopsis?

Q. Is it in order to send the first few chapters of a *novel* to a publisher, with a synopsis of the rest of the novel?

A. Yes, as a matter of fact, most publishers prefer a synopsis, sample chapters, and cover letter rather than the completed novel manuscript. (This is easier on the writer, too, from a postage

Book Publishing Costs

Q. When having a book published, will the author be required to furnish a large sum of money before the book will be published? If you have black and white photographs you want in the book, will these cost extra?

A. Only if the book is to be published by a subsidy publisher will the author have to foot the bill. Regular trade publishers assume all production costs. Photographs usually do increase the cost of putting out a book, and here again, the type of publisher involved (subsidy or regular) will determine who absorbs this extra expense.

Book Forewords—

Q. I can write a good introduction for my book, but because of the theme (importance of proper care in the rapid recovery of mentally ill patients), don't you think it would hold more weight if a psychiatrist wrote the introduction?

A. Yes, an introduction by a psychiatrist would lend more authority to your book. However, this is usually handled by the publisher. In your covering letter, suggest that you know of several prominent psychiatrists who would be willing to write an introduction if the publisher is interested in the book.

Book of Short Stories

Q. Do book publishers put out collections of short novels and stories that haven't previously been published?

A. Yes, but rarely. More often they prefer their collections to be a combination of both published and new stories. For example, in John O'Hara's book, *Assembly*, only ten of the twenty-six stories and short novels, originally appeared in magazines. In the case of an unknown writer, however, the publisher is usually reluctant to bring out a collection of work that has not stood the test of print. It is easier for the beginning writer to establish his reputation through the periodicals, and then try to get a book publisher interested.

Illustrating Books

Q. I am interested in illustrating children's books, but have been unsuccessful in locating any information on the subject. Can you supply me with the information I need? I would like the size of illustrations, medium in which the work should be done, what material should the illustrations be on, etc. I tried to obtain the book by Colby entitled *The Children's Book Field,* only to find it was out of print. Will this book be available at a later date? Are there any similar books on the market?

A. The publisher usually decides exactly what type of illustrations he wants for a particular book. Most publishers of children's books are well acquainted with established local illustrators and will choose the one whose talents are best suited to the specific work at hand. These publishers advise that the artist build experience as a commercial artist with an advertising agency or a printer to learn the graphic art side of preparing illustrations for reproduction, before attempting to enter the children's book field. Illustrations in color are made through the highly technical process of color separations, and the illustrator is expected to have knowledge of this process. The artist should also know the effect of certain book papers on his final artwork; he should be able to work in proportion and follow the publisher's directions for sizes. Once this experience is gained, the artist may then make up a portfolio of his best work, which should include a few things in line, some in two colors, some in full color and in a variety of media. He should then try to get an appointment with a good art director or editor in a juvenile publishing house. Often one of the best ways for the artist to get started in the juvenile field is by having an agent represent him. An agent is constantly calling on the various publishers and knows what type of work they're looking for. He is in a position to recommend whichever of his clients he thinks is best equipped to handle a particular job. Most publishers work strictly on assignment, not speculation. The matter of the size of illustrations, medium, subject matter, etc. for a certain book, would have to be discussed between the publisher and the artist he selects for the assignment. Unsolicited artwork is generally considered a nuisance by the busy publisher and his editors. They also look with disfavor on the book manuscript that arrives with amateurish illustrations done by the author's friend. Authors should allow the publisher to select the illustrator. Additional information about illustration can be found in *Writing, Illustrating and Editing Childrens Books* by Jean Poindexter Colby (Hastings House). The novice illustrator is also advised to get into the habit of looking at children's books in the library, especially the Caldecott winners. As you

can see, this field requires a good deal of specialized knowledge and experience. But remember, too, that publishers are always searching for a fresh new treatment of color and line drawings that say a good deal with just a few strokes of the pen.

Standard Royalty

Q. Can a writer who had never had a book published (but who has sold four stories) get more than ten percent royalties? Is 10% the "usual royalty payment"? How can I insure maximum advances? Can I do better with an agent, both royalty and advance-wise? Can you recommend agents who have been successful with "nonfiction" biographical books and who have been successful in selling them for maximum sums to the movies? The woman about whom I'm writing worked under a name that is not too euphonious. Would you advise me not to use that name? I was planning to use four of the real names of the people who helped her. I have only good things to say about these people. If I use real names, do I have to get permission from these people or permission from their heirs?

A. Ten percent is the usual royalty payment. In order to get the best possible deal as far as royalty and an advance are concerned, it might be advisable to allow an agent to handle the contract negotiations. I suggest that you consult the valuable list of Author's Agents in the latest edition of *Writer's Market*. You will find that in addition to providing names and addresses, this list also indicates those areas, such as nonfiction, in which certain agencies specialize. If the subject of your biography is still alive, check with her on the name she would prefer to have used in the book. But in any case, the euphonious quality of a name should certainly not be a deciding factor in its usage in a nonfiction work. To be on the safe side, get permission wherever possible for the use of those people's real names. When they learn of your project, they will surely be most cooperative.

Book Contract

Q. Does the royalty publisher's clause (on copyright) state that the publisher shall obtain the copyright but that said copyright shall be in the name of the author and shall be that author's property? Where might I obtain an agreement contract from a royalty publisher for observation?

A. Most royalty contracts do set up an agreement whereby the publisher takes out the copyright in the name of the author and assigns it to him. If you glance through a sampling of current best sellers, you'll find that it is the author's name that usually follows the copyright mark. Publishers don't make a practice of sending out sample contracts for study, but since you seem to be mainly concerned about the author's possession of the copyright, you may rest assured that a fair agreement would be reached on that score.

Commercial vs. Subsidy

Q. I have a collection of short pieces, many of which have been purchased and published by periodicals. I plan to offer these for publication in book form and have received letters of release from the periodicals. My question is, if the cost of publishing is borne by the author, can the author own the copyright, or if it is published on a royalty basis, can the author own the copyright?

A. All books published by standard royalty book publishers are copyrighted in the name of the author. Even if the author pays to have the book published through a subsidy publisher, he should require that the book be copyrighted in his name.

Book Distribution

Q. Do you know where I might obtain a list of book distributors? I am having my book printed myself and although I have numerous helpful contacts (publicists, etc.), I want and probably need a distributor.

A. *The American Book Trade Directory* (published by R. R. Bowker Co. and available in most libraries) contains a list of the names and addresses of the major newsstand distributors and book wholesalers whom you might contact about distributing your book.

Textbook Royalties

Q. I would like to know if textbook publishers have a standard royalty schedule. In your August '67 issue, page 75, McGraw-Hill's royalty schedule is published. Does that schedule apply to their textbooks as well as to books in the trade division?

A. No, textbook publishers do not have the same royalty schedule as trade book publishers. College textbooks may vary from 8 to 12% of the *net* price the publisher receives, while elementary and secondary texts may be only 3 to 5% based on the amount of illustration cost and staff work by the publisher.

License to Sell?

Q. I have written a book advocating that the United States should use a three-party political system. I am considering having the book (100,000 words) printed, taking out my own copyright, and distributing the book myself until it realizes a market or dies a fizzle. What kind of license, if any, will I need to sell and distribute my book? And, will you please recommend a reputable and economical printer in the Los Angeles area to handle a paperback edition?

A. I don't know of any specific license you need to sell and distribute your book, but you had best clarify this with your local city officials and the State of California. A list of book manufacturers appears in a directory called the *Literary Market Place* which is no doubt available in your public library.

Second Edition

Q. I published my own book and want a second edition. I plan to send a copy to each of ten publishers. What should I say to them?

A. When submitting a copy of your book to ten different publishers to interest them in a second edition, you should indicate that you are making a simultaneous submission of this book manuscript to a number of publishers and would appreciate a response from them as to whether or not they would be interested in publishing a second edition.

Standard Contract

Q. What is the "standard contract" which book publishers offer to those whose manuscripts are accepted?

A. The standard book contract usually offers 10% of the retail price on the first 5,000 copies sold, 12½% on the next 5,000 copies and 15% on all over 10,000. You might want to check your local library for our *1967 Writer's Yearbook* which contained an excellent article on "What the Beginner Should Know About His First Book Contract."

Free Listings?

Q. I am in the process of publishing my own book. Please inform me as to how I can get "free listings" in all libraries and how can I advertise at an inexpensive rate?

18

A. If you would like to call your book to the attention of librarians, you could do so in a small advertisement in the *Library Journal*, 1180 Avenue of the Americas, New York, N.Y. 10036. You could write their advertising manager to find out what the advertising rates are. The only other way to bring your book to the attention of all librarians would be to send a mailing piece to a list of libraries taken from the *American Library Directory*.

Subsidy Publish?

Q. Should a new writer submit to subsidy publishing houses? Perhaps it might be of some interest to those of us who do have material we'd like to get into print, but are skeptical.

A. Only if a commercial publisher cannot be found to publish your book and you can afford to pay to have your own book published—at a fee which may run into several thousands of dollars— should you as a new writer submit to a subsidy publishing house. If a book is good enough to be published you should send it first to a regular royalty publisher who will pay *you* rather than ask you to underwrite the cost of publishing the book. A comprehensive list of both royalty and subsidy publishers appears in our annual directory, *Writer's Market '69*.

Picture Books

Q. I've written several children's stories that my children really like. I've been

told that I should send them somewhere and get them published. Thanks to *Writer's Digest* I have an idea just where to send them. What I want to know is, How? Also, I want to use a pen name. How do I go about letting the publisher know this?

A. Picture book manuscripts are typed double-spaced with the author's name and address in the upper left corner of the first page of the manuscript. If you wish to use a pen name most writers use this technique: They show their legal name and address in the left corner and then on the title page of their manuscript they show the title of the article, story or book, then the word, "by" and their pen name.

Copy of Contract

Q. Where can I get a copy of the standard Authors Guild Contract?

A. "Your Book Contract," a guide for the use of members of the Authors Guild in the negotiation of contracts with book publishers comes with your membership. Details on eligibility requirements and annual dues are available from The Authors Guild, 234 W. 44th St., New York, N.Y. 10036.

Dedications?

Q. Do book dedications accompany manuscripts when they are mailed to the publisher, or are they added after the manuscripts have been sold?

A. Book dedications are usually submitted by the author after the book has been accepted by the publisher.

Posthumous Work

Q. My husband, a freelance writer, died 2 years ago, leaving numerous stories, several novels and other material which has not been published. I would like to submit the novels to publishers as two of them came very close to acceptance. How do I go about doing this? In other words, must I mention the circumstances when submitting the novel?

A. If the book is accepted by a publisher, you could then explain the situation, since the book contract would have to take into account that you are his legal heir. Don't confuse the issue until that point, however. Just submit the manuscripts for judgment on their own merits.

Rights Offered?

Q. When submitting a book-manuscript to a publisher for consideration, what data concerning "rights" should be attached?

A. It's not necessary to discuss the matter of rights when submitting a book manuscript to a publisher. If they decide to publish the book, the contract they draw up and present to you will have all the rights provisions spelled out. If you agree with them, you can sign the contract; if you don't, you can discuss it further with them before coming to terms.

Multiple Submissions

Q. Can a writer ethically submit copies of a book to more than one book publisher at a time? The system of submitting one copy around to publishers is very inequitable to writers in view of the unreasonably long time many publishers take to report. If a writer could make several copies of a book and submit them simultaneously to a number of publishers, he would have much better odds of locating an interested publisher more quickly. Also, a book might go out of date or another writer come up with a similar idea before an interested publisher saw a manuscript which was dragging around at the rate of one or two submissions a year. Another advantage to a writer's making a number of simultaneous submissions is that it would give him some bargaining power if more than one publisher were interested in the manuscript.

A. There have been a few occasions where writers have used a multiple submission technique for book manuscripts. One example of a writer who did is described in an article in *Writer's Digest's* Feb., 1966 issue. What the writer has to fight, of course, if he submits duplicate copies of the manuscript, is the built-in prejudice of some editors against a manuscript which they know has been submitted not exclusively to them.

Columns Into Book

Q. I have copyrighted some material that I am trying to sell as columns to newspapers. If it is published in the papers and I then want to put the same material into book form, would I have any copyright problems?

A. Although unpublished manuscripts in general cannot be copyrighted, it is possible to copyright a printed syndicated column. As long as you are selling only serial rights to the newspaper columns you have copyrighted, book rights belong to you. The best thing to do when submitting the printed column to the newspapers is to print in the upper right corner of the column, "First North American Serial Rights Only," and remember that the book must acknowledge the copyright date of the periodical publication.

Recipe Book

Q. My sister and I are interested in compiling our collected recipes into a book. Very few are original; most we have collected from newspapers, magazines, books, and friends. We have lost the source of many of them. What are the copyrights for a recipe? Can we legally compile these recipes into a book of our own without securing rights from the creator?

A. Although the listing of ingredients themselves in a recipe cannot be copyrighted, the presentation of the recipe including the directions for preparing the item can be copyrighted. From the cookbooks I have seen, many of whose authors may have faced the same problems you and your sister do, the authors seem to have altered the recipes

slightly by including some other minor ingredient or leaving one out and rewriting the directions so that there is not a word-for-word copy of the material.

Mimeographed Book?

Q. I am working on my first book manuscript. I have it in mind to publish my own book. It will be 80 to 100 pages. I will use letter-size paper folded, making pages about 5½ inches by 8½ inches. Has anyone ever produced a mimeograph paperback book? I know about mimeograph magazines, but I can't recall reading anything about such a book. Can I get a copyright on the mimeographed book? If, after offering it as a mimeographed work, I later wish to have it done by the printer I might choose, would there have to be another copyright?

A. I don't know if anyone has ever produced a mimeographed paperback book, but they probably have. As far as the copyright office is concerned, as long as some printing method has been used that is all that is necessary to qualify the manuscript as a "published work". If you wish to have the mimeographed version redone later by a printer you could obtain another copyright on the revised edition only if there were enough changes in the basic manuscript to qualify it as "a new version". Ask the Copyright Office, Library of Congress, Washington, D.C. for Circular No. 35B explaining this.

Promote a Cookbook

Q. I am planning to write and publish a special cookbook. Can I advertise and sell it with a new products release?

A. You could certainly try your luck with a new products release on your special cookbook. (I'm assuming you have received permission to use any recipes in this cookbook that are not your own.) What success you'd have would depend on how unique the cookbook was and how newsworthy the editors of these new products columns felt it was. Good luck.

More Cookbook Problems

Q. I am working on a cookbook in which I am going to use old family recipes, adapted, of course, to present day materials. I wonder if I need a release form from people from whom I secured recipes since there will be no payment made, other than a copy of the cookbook. If so, would you suggest a form to be used?

A. Yes, it would be a good idea to get a release from each of the people from whom you are assembling recipes for your book and the form you might use in this connection could simply be a statement they would sign something like this: "For value received, I assign the rights to my recipe for '——————' to '——————' for use in her cookbook, '——————'." The "value received" is, of course, the copy of the cook book you're going to give each of the contributors.

Tapes from Book

Q. Some years ago, I wrote a children's book about the whaling era; it included several stories of foreign lands, each having a special song. The book was published in 1956—copyrighted in my name. The book is now out-of-print. As the stories and songs are my own material, I would like to know if I have the right to make tape recordings of them for sale to a publisher who produces visual aids and programs for school use. If there are restrictions to such usage, will you please tell me how I can meet them?

A. Unless the book contract you signed with the original publisher of your children's book about the whaling era reserved to them the right to make tape recordings of them, they are yours to use. These special rights for the use of material contained in books is usually made the subject of a special clause in the contract and you should review the contract to see whether you, or the publisher, or both, share in these rights.

Chapter 5

The Business of Writing

Writers' Attorney

Q. How would I go about finding a competent copyright and literary rights attorney?

A. In about 200 cities throughout the country there are services which will refer you to a qualified lawyer. Such services are sponsored by the local bar associations. If there is one in your area, you'll find it listed in the Yellow Pages of your telephone book under "Lawyer's Referral Service." If there's no such listing, call your local bar association. There is not usually a charge by the service for referring you to a lawyer. There may be a $5-10 consultation fee for a half-hour discussion with the lawyer himself about your question.

Syndicate Payment

Q. When a syndicate is said to pay $25.00, what does this cover? Per column, per idea or for the number of papers that buy the column?

A. Such a flat rate usually refers to the payment for a single feature . . . a one-shot item rather than a continuing column.

Writer's Guild

Q. How can a writer qualify in order to become a member of the Writer's Guild?

A. This organization for professional writers has two branches—one in the East and one in the West. The Mississippi River is the dividing line. The Eastern branch consists of freelance TV writers or staff news writers for radio and TV networks; the Western branch includes these and also screen writers. You must have sold or been employed to write a TV, radio, or movie script within 2 years prior to your application. The initiation fee is $200, and membership dues are $10 a year plus 1% of the writer's income from screen, TV, radio, etc.

Fraudulent Royalty Statement

Q. In an article in *Rogue* (actually about the music business) by Gene Lees is the statement: "Some book publishers cheat the artist with false royalty statements too . . ." Is that true or not?

A. Such defrauding is rare. Most writers accept the statements of publishers in good faith. Many publishers take the precaution of protecting themselves *and* the writer through the following clause in the standard Society of Authors' Representatives book contract: "The Author or his duly authorized representatives shall have the right upon written request to examine the books of account of the Publisher insofar as they relate to the work; such examination shall be at the cost of the Author unless errors of accounting amounting to five (5%) percent or more of the total sum paid to the Author shall be found to his disadvantage, in which case the cost shall be borne to the Publisher."

Pay Your Interviewee?

Q. When you interview a person (not famous) for a feature-type article (human interest) do you agree to pay them for this opportunity? Or do you agree to pay them a certain percentage of the check when (if) it is sold? Perhaps it is not customary to pay them at all. Could you help?

A. In such a situation as you describe, the interviewee would normally not be paid at all. But when you request the interview, explain your project, noting carefully that this article was not assigned to you but that it is something you hope to find a market for. If the interviewee indicates that he will expect payment upon publication of the article (an expectation that's possible but not too probable), you must use your own judgment in determining beforehand whether you wish to do the article under these circumstances and how much of a percentage you would be willing to turn over to him. There are no set fees for this.

What's a Fiction Bestseller Worth?

Q. I would appreciate it if you could tell me how much a book on the fiction bestseller list would bring an author if it were #1 for a period of say a week or a month. Assume the book sells at average price and a standard royalty is paid.

A. The standard minimum royalty payment on trade books is: 10% on the first 5,000 or 10,000 copies, 12½% on the next several thousand copies, and 15% thereafter. The percentage is based on the retail price of the book. As pointed out in "The Economics of a Book" in *Writer's Year Book '66,* a novel that sells 45,000 hardcover copies and is bought by movies, book clubs and paperback house could earn the author $250,000.

Dead and Gone?

Q. How does a writer protect himself from magazines that suddenly "die" leaving one holding the bag for articles published, but not paid for, or retaining manuscripts that will never be returned? It's happened twice since January and the magazines still hold three of my stories. Is there any way to force return of manuscripts and irreplaceable photos?

A. I'm afraid the author doesn't have much recourse when a magazine folds, if he can't locate the publisher. Some publications which do fold make the conscientious effort to return material they've been holding, but others do not and it's almost impossible to force them to return material. You could try writing the Postmaster or Better Business Bureau in the city where they were located.

Time Limit in Contract

Q. I sold an original story and screen play last February. Since the time the contract was signed and my work was taken, the producer who bought it failed to even bother getting in touch with me. He didn't pay me a nickel so far. According to the contract he has to pay only when they start the principal photography, or when the production money is banked. Since there is no time limit in the contract, I wonder if there is any law that protects me in connection with the time element. What could I do if the producer wouldn't be able to raise sufficient money for the production, and consequently, he never would be able to pay me?

A. Unless you had a time limit written into the contract you signed with the producer, (which is always advisable)

I am afraid you do not have much choice except to wait for his ability to line up production money. On the other hand if he has had to abandon the project he may very well be willing to turn back the material to you on request. It is up to you to contact him to see what can be worked out.

Comedy Fees?

Q. An entertainer asked me to show him a few of my skits which take from 15 minutes to a half-hour. How much should the charge be for permitting the performer to use the material and how much should the charge be for selling the material?

A. What you should charge for your material depends largely on how much you can get. Minor entertainers obviously can not pay big fees, while big name entertainers pay their writers fabulous salaries. You might want to look up an article we published in our March, 1965, issue on "Getting Started in Comedy Writing" which may answer a few of your questions, since it describes the activities of a Philadelphia writer starting in a small way.

Fair Fee?

Q. I have been requested to write the life story of a woman who has given me reason to believe she has had unusual experiences that would be worthwhile book material. She feels that since she will relate the episodes and I will write them into an interesting biography, I will be a hired person, somewhat in the capacity of a stenographer, and paid on that basis. I feel that my talent is worth a contract that will guarantee me a 40-60 percentage of the book rights and a percentage on the same basis if the book proves to have other market values. I would like your suggestions on drawing up a contract that would protect both of us fairly.

A. Most freelance writers consider that their talent in writing a book for a subject is certainly worth a fifty-fifty split of the payments. My suggestion is that you draw up a contract detailing what you think is fair to yourself (and the subject) and secure a signature on this agreement before you proceed with any work. For a further discussion of this subject, see "Types of Literary Collaboration" in the October, 1968 *Writer's Digest.*

Newspaper Rates

Q. I would enjoy writing articles, freelance, for the local, small newspapers, but I'm in doubt about the pay received for such material. What is the customary pay for varying lengths of articles?

A. Payment for work contributed to local newspapers is usually by the published inch and it varies from newspaper to newspaper. A typical Midwest daily of 300,000 circulation, pays 40¢ a column inch and smaller papers would pay less.

Trade Magazine Writers

Q. Is there a national association of trade writers?

A. Yes, there is a national association of trade magazine writers. It's called Associated Business Writers of America, and their mailing address is P.O. Box 135, Monmouth Junction, New Jersey 08852.

Full-time Freelance

Q. For many years I've "suffered" with a deep-seated desire to write. But, I guess I've been just too lazy to sit down and get started. Finally, I've come to my senses and have decided to "give in". That's why I'm writing to you. How does a person get started? How does he "break into" the field and make enough to support a family? Perhaps I'm looking for a miracle. The dull routine of the business world is beginning to "bug" me. There isn't even very much money in it unless you know the boss's nephew or second cousin. I want to create and whatever help or encouragement you can offer will be greatly appreciated.

A. I'm afraid if you think there isn't much money in the business world, you will be disappointed too, in how little remuneration there is for the beginning freelancer *until* he develops his talent and his marketing ability. There are hundreds of full-time freelancers, however, who started small and did freelance writing on the side while holding a regular job until they reached the point where they could support themselves and a family on their writing alone. The best place to start, of course, is with articles since the market for them is so much greater than for short stories and there is article material all around every person in every town. Trade Journals are a good place to start. In case you didn't see "How to Sell Your First Article" which appeared in our *1967 Writer's Yearbook,* you might want to consult a copy of that in your local library.

Can an Unknown Sell?

Q. I am a beginner trying to sell juvenile stories and articles. Five months have passed and no sale. Is the juvenile field overcrowded? Would personal letter heads and envelopes help me break through for a first sale? Does it go against my chances to sell because I have never sold?

A. A personal letterhead is not going to influence the sale of a juvenile story or article. A manuscript has to sell itself. You mentioned that you've been trying for five months, but you didn't mention how many submissions that represented. Have you really analyzed your work in light of the types of material these magazine editors are publishing? Can it stand up? If you think your work is good and is marketable by today's editors' needs—don't give up. Keep trying. Good luck!

Reprint Sales

Q. Would you explain how "digest" magazines pay for articles they reprint from other magazines? What percentage does the original publisher get, and what percentage goes to the author? If the author has sold first rights only to the original publisher, does he receive the entire reprint amount? Should he try to sell a reprint of his article to a digest magazine, or do digest editors read most publications and make their own selections?

A. In the digest reprint market payments vary. *Reader's Digest* pays 50% to the original publisher and 50% to the author. *Catholic Digest* and *Children's Digest* pay the publisher and whether the author is paid depends on publishers' policies. When you sell reprint rights to publications other than the digests, you are entitled to the entire reprint fee. But the original publisher does in effect, hold other rights in trust for you, even if he has bought first rights only, until you write and ask that the rights be returned to you.

Ghost?

Q. Could you send me the address of a ghost writer here in New York City?

A. A number of persons offer this type of service for a fee and you'll find their names and addresses in advertisements in *Writer's Digest.* It would be best to write each one and find out what they would charge to work with you.

Syndicates

Q. When I submit a feature to a syndicate, how soon can I expect to hear from them? How can I make sure I get my percentage of the sales?

A. Most of the syndicates listed in the *Writer's Market* say that they will report on submissions in from 2-4 weeks. Some, however, take a couple of months. Unless the sum is large enough to warrant sending an auditor to check the accounts, most writers accept the syndicate's statements in good faith. Publishers and syndicates couldn't stay in business very long if they mistreated writers in this way.

Deductible?

Q. This is in regard to permissible income tax deductions for writers; specifically, the cost of: editorial service prior to submission of a manuscript to a publisher; rent and upkeep of a study; and stationery, postage, and supplies. A query on the above was made via phone to the local I.R.S. prior to including these as deductions on my tax return. After I advised the party at the tax office I had two manuscripts submitted to market through an agent, but none of my work had been published to date, he advised me that I could claim these expenses as allowable. Based on this, I included these deductions in my return, and received the following notice from the Internal Revenue: "Your claims for expenses in connection with your writing is not allowable. These expenses must be capitalized and later de-

ducted over the life of your copyrights." This does not seem right, and there appears to be some confusion, even with the Internal Revenue personnel, on the correct interpretation of the tax law in this regard.

A. The article on tax matters which appeared in *Writer's Digest* in our April 1966 issue, pointed out that the writer must prove only his serious intent to sell his work as a business to claim expenses—whether he has any income from that work in the same year or not. This article was checked for accuracy by the U. S. Internal Revenue Service in Washington, D. C.

Press Credentials

Q. How does a freelance writer (with no official credentials) get a press card, or admittance to sections marked "Press Only"? Our baseball club has been granted a major league franchise but will be playing in the old ball park until the new park is built. Is there any way I can get into the "Press Only" room to take pictures and get personal interviews from the players without lowering myself by rope from above? Or is this one of those situations when a freelance writer is left out in the cold?

A. The best thing for you to do would be to get an advance assignment from some specific magazine or newspaper to do a feature on the baseball club players. You could then present this letter of assignment to the public relations director of the baseball club and gain admittance through him to the players' area. There are no official credentials as such that the individual freelance writer can use. He usually has to ally himself with some specific newspaper, magazine or syndicate market to obtain entry to otherwise restricted quarters such as these.

Press Cards?

Q. Last week, I visited a company to research some information I need in order to finish with a project. Their behavior was very harsh. They said they would not give any information to anybody unless he had credentials proving he is a writer. The same thing happened when I did research work at a museum and at a medical research laboratory. Reporters, telephone operators, merchant seamen, detectives and private investigators and even photographers have identification cards (ID-card-like) to identify themselves. Why not writers? Our job is just as important as theirs! I am sure that the rest of my colleagues feel as I do. Why don't we have a Writers Association to bring together all those interested in the writing field and provide them with the backing, support and benefits of a powerful, non-profit, internationally-recognized organization?

A. There are a great many freelance writers organizations already in existence—and they are designed to meet the needs of specific groups of writers —The Outdoor Writers Association of America, The Science Writers, the Sports Writers, etc. A comprehensive list of these associations with descriptive copy appeared in the August, 1963 issue of *Writer's Digest.*

Business Cards

Q. Having finally gotten a toe in the door with sales to national magazines and California newspapers, I would like to have business cards printed identifying me as a free-lance writer. This would probably simplify introducing myself to people I wish to interview or ask for information. Can you suggest the best wording for such a card?

A. Keep the card as simple as possible, with clear, tasteful lettering. For example, in the center you may have your name and directly beneath it, the words, "Free Lance Writer." In the lower left hand corner, in smaller print, could be your address . . . and in the lower right, your telephone number.

Fair Price?

Q. What do you consider a fair price for writing the historical articles to be published in a commemorative book marking the 100th anniversary of a village? As a freelancer I've sold news and features to the *Evening Bulletin.*

A. Remuneration will have to be based on two factors: 1. What you think the job is worth and 2. What the customer will pay. You will simply have to calculate approximately how much time and effort will be spent on researching and writing these articles, estimate the budget of your client, and then charge accordingly.

Who's the Author?

Q. If a writer buys a plot from an advertised source, or if a writer pays for extensive help in plotting his story or novel, is the finished product legally and ethically his own?

A. In both cases, the finished product belongs to the purchaser who has actually produced the written manuscript, even though he has used the help of others. When there has been extensive help on a novel, it would be ethical to include an acknowledgment in the Foreword or Preface.

Writers' Organizations

Q. I am curious about professional writers' groups like the Authors' Guild, Mystery Writers of America and the Society of American Travel Writers. Are there other general or specialized organizations, say for the authors of juveniles? How do members benefit? What is each group's purpose, scope, present concern? Current membership? Entry requirements?

A. The current addresses of the Authors' Guild, Mystery Writers of America and the Society of American Travel Writers along with detailed answers to some of the other questions you ask appear in the *1969 Writer's Market.*

Sell Ideas?

Q. I would like to know if there is a market in selling ideas to established writers. As an example, say I have what I feel is a powerful plot for a "what if" novel of the *Seven Days In May* genre, but I don't have the Washington political background to make it authentic. Is it possible to sell such an idea to a known writer who has written books with a Washington background? If there is such a market, what is the usual procedure in presentation and payment? Are there any agencies that arrange collaboration between writers?

A. There aren't any agencies which arrange collaboration between writers and unfortunately more people are in the position that you're in—having an idea but not the background to write a book. Those people who do have the background often also have plenty of ideas and aren't in need of such collaboration. The only way this type of collaboration usually works out is if you can find someone in your local area with whom you would like to work.

Chapter 6

Working With a Collaborator

Pay for Life Story?

Q. A friend has offered to relate to me the very unusual story of her life, for use in a novel. The entire writing job will be mine, as well as marketing, etc. I feel she is entitled to some percentage of any profit from the novel. What is the usual percentage in such cases? Am I within my rights to request exclusive use of the material at any later date to use other than for the novel in question?

A. In cases of this type, as well as in biographies, the subject whose life is being used is not usually given any payment except the satisfaction of seeing his life story in print. However, if you feel a personal obligation, why not simply offer a flat sum (whatever is agreeable to both parties) for use of this material, dependent, of course, upon its sale to a publisher. If at all possible, you should secure legal help with any financial arrangement that is made. Since there are others who are probably familiar with the events of your sub-

ject's life, you cannot reasonably expect to have exclusive control over this material. Remember that ideas themselves cannot be copyrighted.

Collaboration Arrangements

Q. An acquaintance has asked me to collaborate in the preparation and marketing of material in the non-technical category. Enough material has been assembled for about 120,000 words, but it is in rough draft form and will need to be rewritten for submission to a publisher. My acquaintance has no knowledge of the mechanics involved so that every bit of the work will be up to me to do. How do I go about being completely fair with her? What agreement should there be regarding money—both profit and preliminary expenses?

A. Collaboration arrangements naturally vary according to the situations and individuals involved. Some collaborators work on a 50-50 basis all the way down the line. You imply that you will be doing most of the work from here on in, so you may feel entitled to a larger percentage, say 60-40, if that is agreeable to the lady. Another alternative might be to agree on a flat sum for your help in preparing the material for submission to a publisher, plus a percentage of the royalties in case of sale. Discuss the matter frankly with your collaborator and if possible, obtain some legal advice that would protect both your rights in this situation.

Friendly? Arrangements

Q. I have been offered the opportunity of collaborating on some stories. A friend of mine went on safari to Africa and took some excellent photographs of his hunting trips. He wants me to write his experiences and he will furnish the photos. If the stories are sold, what percentage do I pay him? Of course all money received for photos would be his, but I have no idea how much I should share with him of the money received for a story.

A. If you are successful in selling some articles to men's magazines for example, and the photographer is paid separately for his photographs, my opinion is that you should receive the entire amount of money for the work you put into the article. There is no set rule of thumb for collaboration fees between writers and photographers. They have to decide when the item is sold how much each person contributed to the sale and make their share of the check reflect that. If the magazine pays the photographer and writer separately, you are relieved of making this decision yourself, since the magazine editor is deciding what proportion of the total check he feels is due each partner.

Collaborating With The Expert

Q. When a writer and an expert in a field (such as an M.D., Ed.D.) collaborate on an article, how are fees received usually divided? I am thinking especially of a situation in which the expert directs the writer to sources of information and reads copy for factual accuracy as his major contribution.

A. There are no set fees between specialists and writers as to what each one's share should be of the payment for an article or book. It just has to be worked out by the individuals based on what percentage of the final sale each person thinks his work contributed. If you think for example that it was your writing that was 75% responsible for selling the article and the expert's contribution 25%, then propose that proportion to the expert. If you think it was a 50-50 deal, suggest that.

Confessions Collaborator

Q. I have some confessions which need revision and I also need help in selling. I would like someone not too expensive but reliable and "on the ball".

A. Some collaborators who have worked in the confession field advertise in *Writer's Digest*. You could write them individually and find out how much they charge for their services.

Chapter 7

Some Questions on Copyright

Copyrighting a Book

Q. What is the approximate cost to copyright a book?

A. The fee for registering a copyright claim is $6.00. Make your check or money order payable to the Register of Copyrights. The address is Copyright Office, Library of Congress, Washington, D.C. 20540.

Copyright Question

Q. I am engaging in some research on fiction writing and wish to use some material in a book. Even though the copyright date is as recent as 1950, the publisher is no longer in business and the author is deceased. The book was copyrighted by the publishing house. Does the book and all its contents now revert to public domain? If not, how do I get permission to use the material?

A. Even though the publisher is not currently in business, he still owns the

copyright which has to run its course of 28 years. You would need his permission to use that material. Contact the U.S. Copyright Office in Washington, D.C. for the most recent address on its records for the copyright owner of this particular book.

Copyright

Q. How does a writer know which magazines will not be copyrighted? Is there a way that I can state on my poems, fillers and manuscripts that I want my work copyrighted? If a writer sells all rights, can he still arrange to have the copyright assigned to him? How can an author obtain a separate copyright?

A. Before you submit a manuscript to a magazine, you should ascertain whether or not that magazine is copyrighted. You can do this easily by obtaining a copy of it and looking for the

33

copyright notice, which usually appears at the bottom of the Table of Contents page. If there is no notice, since you cannot copyright an unpublished manuscript, you would have to obtain certainty of the date of publication, then write for an Application for Copyright to the Copyright Office, Library of Congress, Washington D.C. At the bottom left-hand corner of your manuscript's first page, type your own copyright notice: ©Your name, 1968. As soon as the work is published and available, register your claim by mailing to the Copyright Office in Washington, D.C., the appropriate filled-in Application Form plus one complete copy of the magazine containing your work, and the registration fee of $6.00. If the publisher buys all rights, you may try to arrange with him in advance for the assignment of copyright on your particular piece.

Copyright Symbol

Q. When submitting a manuscript, it is a fact that it is protected until published. However, should the writer place the symbol © *copyright by . . . author's name, all rights reserved* on the manuscript copy? Or is this unnecessary? What is the procedure regarding copyright when submitting a manuscript?

A. It is not permissible to put the copyright symbol and your name on a manuscript that does not have a statutory copyright. Unpublished manuscripts are protected by common law copyright, but they do not carry the copyright symbol. Statutory copyright is available on a certain number of manuscripts—plays for example that have not been published or produced, but a statutory copyright cannot be obtained on an unpublished story, article or poem. Most magazines copyright the entire contents of their publication and if the author wishes the copyright reassigned to her, she must notify the editor in advance and pay the fee to the Copyright Office to have the copyright transferred.

National vs Local

Q. I am interested in syndicating my own newspaper column. Since each newspaper copyrights the material that appears in it, will it be necessary for me to copyright the column in my name in order to send it to several different markets? Also, if the column should appear in a newspaper with a nation-wide circulation, does this mean that I cannot then submit it for consideration to other newspapers with a more limited circulation? If I must copyright the column in my name, how do I go about doing this?

A. Yes, it will be necessary for you to copyright the columns in your own name to protect your rights. This is done by sending a letter, requesting an application form from the Register of Copyrights, Library of Congress, Washington, D.C., and then forwarding the filled-out application form along with a published copy of your column and a check for $6.00 for each column to the Copyright Office. If the column appears in a newspaper with nationwide circulation, yes, you could submit it to newspapers with more limited circulation, but you would have to notify the editors where it has previously been published.

English Translation

Q. I want to write a story in which I would use three verses from *The Rubaiat of Omar Khayyam*. Are his verses, rendered into English by Edward Fitzgerald, in the public domain? My edition says copyright (1938) by the Illustrated Editions Company, Inc. No mention is made of copyright by Edward Fitzgerald.

A. Whether or not the English translation of *The Rubaiyat* which you have, which was copyrighted originally in 1938 has been renewed or not, should be checked out before using the English version. A letter to the Register of Copyrights, Library of Congress, Washington, D.C., could probably determine for you whether or not that copyright is still in effect.

Copyright Expiration

Q. A book passes into public domain after a certain number of years. Since at the time of publication it is not known whether or not reprints will be made at a later date, are the later dates of publication ignored and the original or first date of publication considered with regard to using any material in the book?

A. A copyright can be taken out on a book for 28 years and then renewed once for another 28 years. (Since 1962 copyright expirations have been renewed year by year while the new Copyright Bill is under consideration by Congress.) If the copyright is renewed on a book, subsequent editions of it will show the new copyright date on the fly leaf of the book. If there is any question about whether or not a subsequent edition of a book has been copyrighted —and you have only the original edition at hand—refer to the various Library of Congress directories in your public library, which compile listings of books which have been copyrighted. You could look it up under the title or author to see if it has subsequently been copyrighted.

Humor Collection

Q. For the last fifteen years, or so, I have been collecting jokes, riddles, funny sign slogans, and humorous writings. I've gathered these from friends, acquaintances, therapists, etc. None of them have the author's name, nor whether they were ever published, or anything of this nature that would give me a clue as to their origin. I do not even know if they come under the public domain category. My problem is this. I am attempting to write a book (Probably paperback length, I imagine, incorporating the idea that: a little humor in one's life will make the rough road of rehabilitation a little easier). But since I have no clues as to the author of some of these masterpieces-of-humor, how can I protect myself against possible plagiarism suits?

A. Short gags and jokes can not be copyrighted so you wouldn't have any difficulty in assembling those in a book. Two to three-hundred-word short prose humor pieces, however, might present a problem. If they did appear in originally copyrighted publications, you would have to substantially rewrite them to avoid possible suit for plagiarism.

Book on Copyright

Q. I'm a young writer with work I'd like to send to magazines, but I don't understand about copyrights. I'd like to know the name of a good book explaining copyrights in layman terms.

A. Most libraries should have a book called *A Manual of Copyright Practice* by Margaret Nicholson (Oxford) which is a good basic reference source.

Copyright Unknown

Q. Does it cost anything to have the Copyright Office look up to see if a certain old book is still copyrighted?

A. The Library of Congress has a search fee of $5.00 per hour to search whether or not a book has a current copyright on it and most searches take at least an hour or two. For further information on the subject of the book in question, you might write to the Registrar of Copyrights, Library of Congress, Washington, D.C. 20540.

Radio Material

Q. What is the copyright status of Radio Broadcast Material (helpful hints, short features, poetry, recipes, etc.)? Can this material be re-used verbatim, or otherwise under what restrictions?

A. Although radio and television were not specifically covered by the Copyright Act, some material presented thereon—dramatic scripts for example, are copyrighted in that form. For a more comprehensive explanation of copyright, and its application to radio and TV, you might want to look in your local public library for a book called *A Manual of Copyright Practice* by Nicholson.

Newspaper Column

Q. What copyright protection do I have on material used in my weekly newspaper column on sewing? A friend of mine would like me to use some of her ideas in my column, giving her credit. Would she receive any copyright protection?

A. Unless the newspaper as a whole or your column in particular is copyrighted, there is no protection for the material used in it. This applies to your friend's items as well as your own. If you want to get all future columns copyrighted in your name, write for further information, to the Copyright Office, The Library of Congress, Washington, D.C. 20540.

Copyrighted Art?

Q. Is advertising art and lettering in national magazines copyrighted? What I have in mind is using some text and photos and drawings from parts of different ads, combining them in a paste-up to be photographed and printed as an original work.

A. Such work is copyrightable, so you'd better get permission before you start cutting and pasting.

A. The American copyright law as it currently exists is this. A book may be copyrighted for a period of 28 years and then renewed for another period of 28 years. Since a new copyright law is currently under consideration in Congress, legislation has been passed since 1962 automatically renewing copyrights which might expire in these last few years for one more year to bring them up to the period at which the new copyright law might take effect.

Submitting Maps

Q. I have a travel article in preparation now for which I will need maps as part of the illustrations. I don't know what kind of map to submit. What about copyrights in reproducing from maps?

A. Maps are copyrightable, so permission would be necessary to reproduce a previously published, copyrighted one. Submit the map you think best for your article along with copyright owner's address where the editor can write for reprint permission if he decides to use.

Copyright Law

Q. I would like any information I can get regarding the Copyright Law on books.

Chapter 8

What Do They Mean By . . . .?

Definitions of Terms

Q. Beginning writers are usually advised to try to sell their writing to the "little magazines" rather than the bigger and better known ones. My problem is this: Which ones are the "little magazines" and where may I obtain a list of them?

A. There is a difference between "little magazines" and "lesser known" magazines. This distinction has to do with the fact that in literary circles, the term "little magazines" refers primarily to those publications, frequently put out by universities, which, though often nonpaying, do print works of high literary caliber and social consciousness. This group includes such magazines as *Arizona Quarterly, Alabama Review, The Literary Review,* etc. Beginning writers are not usually advised to slant toward these quality markets, but toward those little-known magazines which do not pay as much as the top slicks, for example, but which do use

similar material. You will find a comprehensive list of all these publications, complete with current data on payment rates, theme preferences, etc., under such various categories as "miscellaneous general," "religious magazine," "trade journal," etc., in the latest edition of *Writer's Market,* a helpful book that may be ordered directly from *Writer's Digest.*

The Freelance

Q. When is a person considered a freelance writer? Someone told me if I had at least one article published that I was considered a freelance writer. Is this true?

A. Freelance means that the person is self-employed as a writer and is not on the salaried staff of any one newspaper, magazine or publishing house. Some writers who have published little still consider themselves freelancers because they are working on their own and submitting to the markets of their choice. The professional's viewpoint is that a true freelance writer earns a substantial part of his income from his writing.

Writers' "Average" Income

Q. Every so often I see something about the average salary of the writer in America. But just who is this writer? The income mentioned is so low that I cannot see how the supposedly high-priced TV and movie writers can be included in this average. And is the average writer someone like me who works full-time at another job and has never sold anything for more than fifteen dollars?

A. Such an "average salary" is presumably arrived at by a study of the incomes of all types of writers. Since there are so many more part-time and low-earning writers (like yourself) than there are top TV and screen writers, it is not hard to see why the resultant "average" income is not very high.

Tear Sheets

Q. If you quote a title and some verses from a song in a short story (with permission, of course) and the publishing company who holds the copyright asks for a "tear sheet" if the story is published, what exactly is it that you send?

A. If and when the story is published, you would simply clip (or "tear") the appropriate pages out of the magazine and send them to the publisher who requested such "tear sheets."

Offbeat Poetry

Q. What can I say? I have a poetry column in a local journal. Some of my recent poetry is unrhymed and has no regular rhythm. Readers constantly hound me with the comments, "That's a poem?" or "It doesn't rhyme!" or "It has no set rhythm!" The truth of the matter is, I have sold more so-called "offbeat" poetry than the "perfect" poem. What can I say to my readers?

A. Tell them you are writing free verse . . . because that *is* what you're doing. Point out to those readers that this is an accepted literary tradition, followed by Walt Whitman and T. S. Eliot, to name just two. No apologies are necessary!

Filler Markets

Q. I would like to know what is meant by fillers. Where would a writer get this material?

A. Fillers mean what their name implies. They may be crossword puzzles, newspaper clips, short featurettes, poetry, brief anecdotes, sayings, etc., that are used to fill up the empty spaces left in the magazine layout after the regular features have been placed in position. The type of filler would depend on the slant and makeup of the magazine. Fillers may either be original or they may be quoted from other sources. In the case of the latter, the original source and date of publication is indicated by the writer when submitting. Hundreds of the magazines buying fillers describe their needs in the *Writer's Market*.

Syndicates

Q. What is a "syndicate"? How does it serve a writer of factual articles?

A. A syndicate is a business service that makes a wide variety of features available to many publications. A newspaper syndicate, for example, might sell the same column to different newspapers all over the country. Each newspaper would pay for this column according to the size of its circulation. A nonfiction writer might be interested in selling a daily or weekly column to a national syndicate on a royalty basis. For a description of the editorial needs and the names and addresses of syndicates, see *Writer's Market* or you may purchase (for $2.00) a Syndicate Directory from *Editor and Publisher,* 850 Third Ave., New York, N.Y. 10022, which lists all syndicated features presently being sold.

Pedestrian Writing

Q. Several times I have come across literary criticism using the phrase "pedestrian writing." The phrase has been used in discussing published material without stating whether or not it is considered good writing. Exactly what is "pedestrian writing" and what makes it so?

A. The term "pedestrian," when applied to writing, is definitely unflattering. It means that the work is prosaic or dull. The Latin root "ped-" refers to the foot, and of course the usual definition of the noun "pedestrian" is: one who travels on foot . . . such as the common man (who presumably doesn't have a fancier way to travel). In connection with writing, the adjective then would mean common or ordinary.

Newspaper Stringers

Q. What is the definition of the word "stringer" as used in the following ad: "Newspaper chain has opening for editor and also has openings for stringers in all sections of the country." Are they the same as correspondents or different? Please explain.

A. Yes, A stringer is a local correspondent whose job it is to keep his regional newspaper supplied with items concerning his particular community. The term is an old newspaper one that derives from the fact that a local correspondent's copy was strung together, measured, and then paid for by the inch. If you're interested in learning more about stringers, read the article entitled "How to be a Small Town Stringer" by Reinhart Wessing in Aron Mathieu's *The Creative Writer.*

"Quality" Magazine

Q. Specifically what is a "quality magazine"?

A. Specifically, *Atlantic, Harper's, Esquire, Saturday Review,* etc. The magazines in this "quality" group have high literary standards and are interested in the artistic merit of the writer and his ability to express himself in a sensitive and individualistic manner. Fiction is usually of the nonformula type, and the emphasis is frequently on characterization and insight into human emotion and behavior rather than on the intricacies of plotting.

Those Trade Terms!

Q. What is a "think piece"? Does it mean a controversial article? Or does it mean all kinds of nonfiction? Even a historical piece, non-controversial, will cause me to think—and doubtless most other readers.

A. A "think piece" is usually any article that has an intellectual, philosophical, provocative approach to its subject.

Mailing Services

Q. What does "mailing and remailing" mean in the ads in your magazine?

A. A mailing service agency mails an author's work from its own locality when the author travels frequently or prefers a postmark that does not reveal his place of residence.

Story or Article?

Q. When a story is based on an actual happening, but polished up to a degree, should it be called a story or an article? In today's writing, the dividing line between fiction and fact is so narrow it is hard to distinguish between them.

A. If a story is told from the first-person viewpoint and the incidents are factually accurate and based on a true personal experience, with just enough elaboration to make them more dramatically effective, the story would probably be considered nonfiction, of the type used by many men's magazines, e.g., *Man's World, Saga, True West, etc.*

"Newsbreak"?

Q. What I would like to know is what are "newsbreaks"? Editors think everyone knows everything there is to know about making a buck in this freelance field and every so often I run into such phrases which really make me wish for a beginner's book or dictionary on writing. Is there such a guide so I can look up terms that "stump" me?

A. A "newsbreak" to most editors is simply a newsworthy event or item. For example, an opening of a new retail shoe store in a town might be a "newsbreak" for a shoe trade journal that published news items of new openings. A glossary of some other publishing terms appeared in the September, 1968 issue of *Writer's Digest.*

Writing in "Depth"

Q. Would you explain the term "depth" in the field of writing?

A. "Depth" would naturally mean many things to many editors. But perhaps the one interpretation they would all agree on is that a piece of writing that has depth has something important to say to readers. It would avoid frivolity or top-of-the-head superficiality about the ideas presented; it would require thought on the part of the writer *and* the reader. Nonfiction of depth would be based on well-researched data. Fiction of depth would arise from thoughtful sensitivity to and perception of human behavior.

Amateur vs. Professional

Q. When editors say they want professionally written or sophisticated stuff, what do they mean?

A. They mean they want the type of writing that represents a polished use of the language plus skillfully developed treatment of the subject. Flaws in grammar and word choice, lacklustre style, sloppy plotting or research, poor organization, absence of a point, all are signs of the amateur rather than the professional. The demand for sophisticated material rules out anything trite or corny but suggests a desire for a certain degree of wit and subtlety that would have appeal for readers who are intellectually sharp about the significance of the world around them.

Contributor's Copies

Q. Is not the phrase, "Payment in contributor's copies" ambiguous? Does it not mean in copies to contributors?

A. "Contributor's copies" is a term that is generally taken to mean copies of the issue in which the contributor's work appears.

Help!

Q. What is a "pot-boiler"?

A. This term refers to something done only for the money, that is, *to keep the pot boiling*. The writer who turns out work of little or no artistic merit just so he can earn a living may be said to be producing "pot-boilers."

Chapter 9

Getting Along With Editors

Acknowledge Acceptance?

Q. When a manuscript is accepted for publication, should you make any response to the editor—or your correspondent? (Such as "Hooray!") If so, when? On acceptance, on receiving your check, or on publication?

A. Though a response isn't mandatory, if your overwhelming joy, gratitude or surprise needs an outlet, by all means write a note when you learn of your manuscript's acceptance. The editor will be glad you're glad.

They Changed My Story

Q. I wrote a piece for a certain magazine. It took a year before it was published. But when it did come out, well, they spelled my name right, but that was about it. The style was hacked apart until there was no style: What's more, facts were altered, so the reader was bound to get an impression different from what I had intended. Is it possible for an unknown to get the last word on what gets printed and what changes are to be made?

A. It would be unusual for an unknown writer to get final approval of his altered story. However, if you don't mind jeopardizing a possible sale, you could try to negotiate for this right by mentioning it when first submitting your mss.

How Long?

Q. How long may a publisher hold a manuscript? I submitted an unsolicited article to a professional magazine in March 1967, was told in March 1968 to be patient for another few months, but the article would be published soon, probably in July. Fee was not discussed. Now it's August and I wonder, since this is my first piece that ever came this close, how long should I be "patient"?

A. If an editor has accepted an article and it hasn't appeared within 18 months, it is reasonable for the writer to inquire of the editor whether it will be published and if not you would like to resubmit it elsewhere.

Pressure Point?

Q. Does it cause raised eyebrows in editorial departments when we use air mail to help speed things along? The other day I received an article back within a week without so much as a rejection slip. Could my air mail postage have made the first reader feel, "Well, if she's in *that* much of a hurry, I'll send it back quickly so she can send it to someone else."?

A. It's doubtful that air mail postage would hamper the sale of a manuscript. Eyebrows would be raised only if the article arrived at the editor's desk with postage due!

Story Acceptance

Q. If a story should be accepted by a magazine, what happens? Does the writer just get a check in the mail or are there preliminaries to go through, such as signing some paper that the writer is the originator of the story, rights, etc.?

A. The writer is customarily notified of acceptance by mail. The check may be included or may follow later, depending on the policy of the publisher. The rights being offered for sale are usually specified by the writer on the manuscript itself (in the upper right hand corner of page 1) and the publisher assumes the writer is the story's originator, so there is rarely any paper to sign to this effect. If the writer has any specific questions about rights, he should make them known to the publisher before cashing the check.

Editors Explain Rejections?

Q. After four years of free lance writing and not having sold a word, I would already be content with only a personal remark from an editor on why the ms doesn't qualify, instead of the usual cold-blooded rejection slips. Is there a special approach you can recommend?

A. Most new writers need objective help in discovering the flaws that prevent their work from selling. But only frustration results from expecting this help from the wrong party. An editor's job is to find publishable material, not to explain rejections. Considering the thousands of manuscripts that yearly cross an editor's desk, such personal analyses would be impossible from the time standpoint alone. What you want is a criticism service, such as the Writer's Digest Criticism Department, which offers detailed critiques at reasonable rates. (See page 68)

SASE with a Query?

Q. Should one always send a self-addressed stamped envelope with a query letter? After receiving a favorable reply to a query, how soon would the editor expect the manuscript?

A. Yes, it's always a good idea to send a self-addressed, stamped envelope with the query letter. When an editor gives you a go-ahead on an article idea and doesn't specify any specific time in which he'd like to see the manuscript, then it's up to you to decide how quickly you can get it finished and acknowledge his letter with a note saying when you will deliver the article.

Editor—Author Relations

Q. As the editor of a literary magazine, do I have the right to make changes in accepted manuscripts? With or without the author's approval?

A. It would be good practice for an editor to discuss any *significant* changes with the author.

What Do They Mean?

Q. I keep getting personal letters from editors to the effect that "It's interesting but not quite right for us." What does this kind of statement mean? If it's so interesting, why isn't it right?

A. These letters' expression of interest is meant to encourage you, to show you that your work does have a degree of promise. However, the material's style or content may not be in keeping with the editorial requirements, or something similar may have recently been published. Get to know the markets better by studying what these publishers *are* buying.

Resell Same Article?

Q. If I sell an article with pictures to one magazine, can I sell the same article again to another magazine?

A. If the first magazine bought first rights only, then yes, you can resell. If you attempt to resell the piece after the first magazine buys and *before* they print it—you will, of course, have to be sure you're completely reslanting the piece so that the editor who bought first rights will have no cause for complaint

if the articles should be published simultaneously. It's always safest to advise the second editor that another aspect of this subject was treated by you in an article bought by such and such a magazine, since he may feel the two publications are in competition even though you don't.

Visit the Editor?

Q. As a novice, unpublished writer, I would like to know if one must usually go see the fiction editor personally.

A. A writer should not visit the fiction editor at all. It is best to send in the manuscript by mail, and include a self-addressed stamped envelope for its safe return in case it's not published.

Did He Mean It?

Q. Recently, a manuscript was returned by an editor who had previously taken ten of my stories. He wrote, "Although we like your story quite a bit, we unhappily have no space left for the current publishing year's issues. We will, however, be considering manuscripts again along about New Years for next year." Would I be justified in holding my manuscript until January and submitting it again?

A. Take him at his word and resubmit your story, perhaps with a tactful note reminding him of how much he liked it. If he had meant to flatly reject it, it isn't likely he would have added that sentence about considering manuscripts the first of the year.

Rubber Stamp?

Q. Every time a writer submits a story he, in effect, is obliged to extend to the publisher what amounts to an option ad infinitum on the manuscript. How about my getting a rubber stamp made: "This manuscript is offered to you for sale, with an option of purchase terminable in thirty days from date." What would the customer (publisher) have to say about something like that?

A. That depends on the customer. There are book publishers, for example, who normally take about 90 days to report on a manuscript, so in such a case, your rubber-stamped 30-day ultimatum might bring your manuscript back unread. However, in most cases, particularly with magazine submissions, there should be no objection to such a stamped statement provided it allows a reasonable length of time for consideration of the manuscript. Summon up your patience and try offering 60 days instead of 30.

No Name, No Pay!

Q. When a magazine advertises payment of a set sum per word, shouldn't they be expected to pay it? True, it was only a six-line verse filler, but they did use it! I received no letter of acceptance or rejection. To add insult to injury, they didn't even use my name. How can I be sure this won't happen again to some longer, more important piece?

A. Perhaps you forgot to put your name and address on your manuscript, as you did on this letter to us! But in any event, you are entitled to write to that editor, asking why you received neither by-line nor the advertised payment. To be sure this won't happen again, don't submit any future material to this publication ... and before you send in to other magazines, you might ask them about their rate of payment for fillers.

Paid But Unpublished

Q. Is it "cricket" to ask when one might expect something to see print? I've had a number of manuscripts accepted (and paid for) but to my knowledge they have not been published.

A. A tactful query on your part certainly seems in order here to end the suspense. But bear in mind that sometimes, for one reason or another, a paid-for piece never does get into print.

Forgotten Author?

Q. I'm mystified! Once in awhile I sell a story which the magazine pays for yet I never see it in print even though they say they will send copies of their magazine containing it. I'm in hopes you can give me some advice or helpful ideas explaining this situation, as I'm typically egotistical enough to want to see my 'brainchildren' in published form.

A. Sometimes magazine editors just forget to send out copies of stories they published to the original authors and my suggestion is that you just drop a note to each one of the magazines involved and ask whether or not your story has appeared so that you could receive a copy of it. In a few other cases either editors change or editor's policies change and although stories are bought it is decided not to use them. It certainly wouldn't hurt however to clarify the situation in each case of your stories.

Lost Manuscript

Q. Is a magazine publisher responsible for stories that he received but which were apparently lost in his office? One of my stories was lost by one of the major magazine publishers. I have a letter from them stating that they cannot find it, and I am wondering if I should ask them to pay for it, inasmuch as I cannot send it elsewhere.

A. Many magazines go on record as indicating they are not responsible for unsolicited manuscripts so that legally they can not be charged.

Plagiarism?

Q. In December, I submitted an article to a new magazine. The following February, I received a rejection slip with the note: "We are quite taken with your style and would appreciate receiving material from you in the future." I was thrilled even with the rejection in this manner. The next August issue of this particular magazine appeared on the newsstand, bearing an article by the same title. Though the printed article is admittedly better than my submission, being longer and more thoroughly re-

searched, it is similar beyond belief. The title, style, opening and closing paragraphs and the content are almost identical. It is hard for me to accept this as coincidence. Do I have any right to question this similarity?

A. Many writers get the same idea at the same time and often use the same language in writing up their ideas. But, if you think there was some appropriation of your material, I certainly would write the editor and question him or her on the article which appeared in the August issue which was so similar to the one you submitted in December.

Legal Recourse?

Q. After reading the outline of my proposed historical novel, a leading publisher asked me to mail Prologue and four chapters. The manuscript was mailed, *first class* postage enclosed for return. The publisher acknowledged receipt. I did not hear from the publisher again. After approximately three months I wrote a letter inquiring as to their decision. The Editorial Department replied that my manuscript had been misfiled; that they did not know it had come in until receipt of my letter. Within a few weeks the senior editor wrote a rather vague letter saying the chapters had not lived up to the outline; that the manuscript was being returned *fourth class*. More than two and one-half months have passed and the manuscript has not been received. The publisher says they have asked the Postoffice Department to trace it. If the

Postoffice is unable to locate it, as now seems possible, do I have recourse against the publisher? There's something illogical about the publisher's explanation.

A. I do not believe you have much recourse against the publisher who has returned your manuscript and from whom you have not yet received it. It is an unfortunate experience but I think you are probably unduly suspicious of the publisher. As a professional author you undoubtedly kept a carbon copy of the manuscript so it would simply be a matter of retyping the four chapters that had been sent to them.

Withdraw Material?

Q. Three months ago, I sent some of my best poems to a certain publisher, who never acknowledged them. Anxious to put them back into circulation, I requested their return, a little less than two weeks ago. My letter was not acknowledged; neither have the poems been returned. I had, of course, sent the usual stamped envelope when I sent the verse in February. My query is this: may I legitimately write the editor in question stating that I withdraw my offer of the poems and then send them to other editors? Inasmuch as a number of my other verses, no better than those I had sent out in February, have been accepted, I should like to offer the latter for publication.

A. Yes, the procedure is to send the publisher a registered or certified letter indicating that you are withdrawing from their consideration the poems mailed them on such and such a date, and then list the titles of the poems. You are then free to resubmit this material elsewhere.

What Mailing Method?

Q. So many times in the last few years when I sent in stories or articles with photos by the Special Fourth Class Rate—Manuscript, with the postage for that rate, my manuscripts were returned to me by First Class, the added postage applied and my own directions crossed out and the First Class stamped on my return envelope. Is it that editorial policy frowns on the cheaper rate and am I obligated to reimburse the editor? If a writer is sending out a good many manuscripts, new or revised stories, regularly then the Fourth Class Rate is certainly a big help when finances are hard to come by. The price of paper and photo-finishing has gone up so the saving has to come from somewhere, via cheaper postal rates. Editorially speaking, do I downgrade my own stuff by using the Fourth Class Rate?

A. The fact that some of your manuscripts are returned by magazines first class instead of special fourth class rate is to your advantage just because it happens to be the magazine's policy and you certainly aren't under any obligation to reimburse the editor. The special fourth class rate is an advantage for the writer who is making a great many submissions, especially of packages containing photographs, etc., and you do not downgrade your material by sending it at that rate. Editors are understanding about the financial problems of freelance writers and rea'ize it is only being professional to do it the least expensive way.

Magazine and Book Marketing

Q. While my nonfiction book is circulating among publishers, may I try to sell parts of it as magazine articles? If so, how do I mark the article mss? the book ms? If I mark an article ms *First Rights,* what happens if the book is published before the article is printed? Some of my articles have lain in editors' files for years before coming to light.

A. Yes, you should mark your article manuscripts "First Serial Rights Only" while your nonfiction book is circulating among publishers. If you do subsequently sell the book, and it is published before an article you have also sold sees the light of day, then you should write the magazine editor and explain the circumstances. Since they would, in effect, only be buying "Second Serial Rights," at that point they may wish to ask that a portion of their payment be returned.

Nudge Editor?

Q. To the unestablished writer, marketing becomes as difficult, or more so, than the creative effort. My particular problem is trying to place timely or seasonal material. The classic example was a Christmas poem I mailed in August

to a top publication which was returned the following February. There was no acknowledgment of a letter I had written to say I was sending the poem elsewhere. Would sending topical material registered mail help, or would this antagonize an editor?

A. When sending topical material, just include in a covering letter a brief request that since the material is timely would the editor try to give reply on the ms by such and such a specific date. This won't help in every case, but it may reduce your frustrations with a few editors.

Free Critique?

Q. Can editors be counted on to give authors any hints as to *why* their stories fail to sell?

A. Whether editors will give advice to authors on why they are rejecting stories—the answer is that some will and some won't, depending on the time they have available to offer this kind of personal criticism to writers who they feel hold future promise. Unfortunately most editors are so harrassed by too much work and so little time that they are not able to provide this service.

How Long To Wait?

Q. What is the reasonable amount of time one should wait for a purchased article to be published? I sold an article to a monthly publication a year ago, was paid for it, but it has not yet appeared in print. The material could be slightly dated by now. If a magazine purchased a piece and then decided not to use it, would they return it to me? Would I then be obligated to return the money (long since spent, of course)?

A. In the "Code of Ethics" *Writer's Digest* published for writers and editors in its January 1966 issue, we suggested that if a magazine had not published material it had bought within 18 months, the writer should feel free to ask the magazine to return it for republishing elsewhere and be permitted to retain the original fee paid for it. This guide line is also used by the Society of Magazine Writers and you might mention both of these items to the publisher you plan to write about your own submission.

Multiple Query

Q. My partner and I have collaborated on a children's book. She is doing the text and I am doing the illustrating. We sent several query letters to different publishers to see if they were interested in the material. We received a letter from a publisher who said he would like to see the material immediately so we sent it out to him. In the meantime we have received answers to all our letters, all saying they are interested and would like to see the material. Can you tell us the best way to answer these letters? Also, can you tell us approximately what the going rate is on a book of this type? Approximately what can the writer expect to receive and what does the illustrator receive?

A. As to what to say to the other publishers who have asked to see your book, all I can suggest is that you write each one saying that your manuscript is currently in the hands of another publisher and, as soon as it is returned, you will send it on to them. As for royalties, they range from 10-15% with splits between author and illustrator varying depending on amount of work by each.

Chapter 10

Education For Writers

Education

Q. How valuable is a college education or at least some college training to a writer? I am interested primarily in fiction and feature writing. Is a good non-college correspondence course from a reputable writers school sufficient?

A. Creative writing courses, whether at college or through a reputable correspondence school, are valuable in helping the beginning writer master fundamental techniques, polish his style, and gain insight through constructive authoritative criticism of his work. They are not sufficient in themselves. A broad general education, whether acquired formally at college or informally by other means, is necessary too.

Grammar Phobia

Q. I am a "would-be" writer; that is, I believe I could write salable material if I could only get rid of one great big fear—the fear of punctuation! Just how important is punctuation to the sale of

a story or article? I have read and studied the English grammars till I feel positively hopeless when I can't remember the rules a minute after I've closed the book. I'm desperate when I can't recall the rule for using a semi-colon, a period, a comma, or when to start a new paragraph. I waste more time trying to decide where a comma goes, or whether to use a semi-colon, or to start a new sentence. Like I said, I can't remember the rules! Are all writers expert grammarians? Should I let this fear stop me from trying to write?

A. You have let punctuation become more of a bugaboo than it really should be for you. Notice your punctuation in this very letter . . . it's quite acceptable. You probably used common sense as your guide. You properly allowed a semi-colon to separate two principal clauses. You used the comma to indicate pauses in a train of thought and to separate the words in a series. You used the period to denote the end of a statement. Since you're allergic to books of rules, perhaps you would do better to work with the stories published in current magazines. Become aware of the function of punctuation by seeing how it's used in each case. By all means, continue to write and never let your fear of literary mechanics scare you off. If the talent is there, it will be recognized whether or not a comma is in the right place.

Journalism Departments

Q. Could you tell me the rank or list of the top ten or fifteen journalism departments in our universities?

A. There is no definitive list concerning the academic standing in journalism. However, your public library undoubtedly has the booklet, "Programs in Journalism," which is put out by the American Council on Education for Journalism and which does list, in alphabetical order, all the Accredited Schools and Departments of Journalism on the college level. For additional information, address your inquiry to: John E. Stempel, Secretary-Treasurer, American Council on Education for Journalism, Dept. of Journalism, Ernie Pyle Hall, Bloomington, Indiana.

"Best" School?

Q. Can you send me a listing of the *best* creative writing schools for would-be novelists?

A. Which is the "best creative writing school" for you would depend on what you expect from it, how much you can afford to pay, your own talents, and

many other factors. Each year, the September issue of *Writer's Digest* publishes a list of schools throughout the country which offer creative writing courses. The only thing you can do is write a few of them and ask for specific details, and then make your own decision.

Fellowships, Grants

Q. I would appreciate it if you would direct me to a list of known literary fellowships and grants, connected with publishers, colleges, etc.

A. A comprehensive list of writers fellowships, grants and foundations appeared in the January, 1960 issue of *Writer's Digest*. A number of current grants also appeared in the September and October, 1966 issues. Continuing news on the subject appears in the "Contests and Awards" column of *Writer's Digest*.

"Best" School of Journalism?

Q. My son is now finishing his first two years at our local junior college and is ready to go on to a four-year institution. He wishes to major in journalism. We can't seem to find any information on what is considered to be the best school of journalism.

A. Which is the "best" school for your son depends on what he wants to specialize in, what you can afford, and many other factors. Many employers consider the product—the person himself as the most important thing to consider—not necessarily where he went to school. You might, however, want to study a paperback book for further information on various colleges, and it's called *The Comparative Guide to American Colleges,* published by Harper & Row, and it sells for $2.95.

Scholarships and Loans

Q. I am a high school Senior and am planning on entering a college next fall. The field I am interested in is journalism. Would you please give me information on journalism pertaining to scholarships, and loans?

A. Information on the scholarships, fellowships and loans available to students can be secured for ten cents from the National College Student Foundation, Inc., 706 South Hartford St., Kennewick WA 99336.

Chapter 11

How To Submit Fillers

One At a Time?

Q. For selling filler items, is it wiser to send in one item at a time in either letter form or on a postcard? Do editors object to getting such items from writers trying to make money?

A. It's all right to submit several filler items at one time. But each should be double-spaced on a separate full-size sheet of paper. If the material is suitable for an editor's needs, he'll be happy to be helping along a struggling writer.

Fillers to Resell

Q. I recently bought some bound volumes of old magazines . . . *The Youth's Companion* (dating from 1897 through 1908). There are many perfectly delightful human interest fillers. How could I best use them . . . If I could use them at all? Could I rewrite and bring them up to date to fit our more "modern" humor?

A. Since these fillers are now in the public domain, you may indeed use them however you wish. You could modernize them and try to sell them individually, or as part of a collective article.

Fillers

Q. Evelyn P. Johnson in her article, "How to Sell Fillers" in the November '66 *Writer's Digest* says that she rewrites unusual news stories to submit to other markets. She says there are no laws against using and reusing ideas culled from newspapers. Does this apply to by-lined feature articles as well?

A. While news items are facts open to anyone's interpretation, feature articles usually have a specific slant or angle, and involve the research, selectivity and interpretations of the individual writer. These are protected by the overall copyright on the paper.

Resubmitting Fillers

Q. When is the writer safe in resubmitting fillers to other magazines after not receiving an acknowledgement or a return of his material from the first magazine he tried?

A. Unless the magazine gives a specific reporting time (such as *Reader's Digest* which mentions eight weeks), if three months go by without a word, you should feel free to resubmit.

A. The sheet is preferable to the index card, and your name and address should be included in standard manuscript form. A covering letter is not necessary.

Re-use Fillers?

Q. As a beginning writer I am considering submitting some children's sayings and anecdotes as fillers in an effort to earn expenses while getting started in the writing field. My question is, will it be ethical to use any of these that might be sold for publication in longer articles at a later date or will I no longer be free to use them at all. Some of them are personal experiences.

A. Whether or not you could use the children's sayings you are planning to submit as fillers in longer articles at a later date, would depend on what rights the magazines to whom you sent the fillers bought. If they bought all rights, you have problems. If they only bought first rights to the material they publish in their magazine, then you would, of course, be free to use the material elsewhere again.

Submitting Fillers

Q. When sending epigrams, gags, etc. to magazines, is it "professional" to send it on 8½ × 11 sheets—or can you send it on index-size cards? Should you put your name, address and word count on the top as you do for large material? What about a covering letter?

Chapter 12

Legal Problems of Writers

Same Title?

Q. The title of a short story that is currently appearing in a magazine is the exact title I wish to use for the title of my first novel. Could there be any complications in such a situation if my novel were published under the same title?

A. Since titles alone can't be copyrighted, your book title's similarity to the story's title should not cause any trouble.

Actual Company Names

Q. Can a writer use the actual name of a business firm in fiction when it doesn't reflect uncomplimentarily on the business without running into trouble, legally or otherwise?

A. Well-known companies such as Macy's or Marshall Field would not look unfavorably on a little free advertising imbedded in a nationally distributed piece of fiction, provided such usage is strictly for purposes of atmosphere and realism. Nothing even remotely illegal or distasteful should be

connected with the company name. For example, if your story deals with a criminal who dupes a department store, you'd be on safer ground if you used a fictitious company name, to avoid the possible impression that the real store is not smart enough to escape being duped. As a rough rule of thumb, when in doubt, fictionalize ... or else hire a smart lawyer.

Invasion of Privacy?

Q. A neighbor of mine, who is disfigured from the hips down, is a recluse. I have built an interesting story around such a woman, saying she became this way because of an auto accident at which time her lover was killed; she had been about to be married. I slander her in no way, yet my husband feels I will have a lawsuit on my hands if the story gets published. I would appreciate any advice.

A. It would be best to change as many of the obvious true-to-life-facts as possible. Give your heroine a different age, size, hair coloring, nationality, etc. Add new mannerisms, idiosyncrasies, other aspects of personality. Use a totally different setting if you can. After all, the only basic idea you need is that of a disfigured recluse. It is not necessary to make the type of disfigurement identical to that of your neighbor. Use your creative imagination to produce a completely new individual based on the general idea but not the exact details of your neighbor's life. In fact, you might even experiment with the idea of making the leading character a man instead of a woman.

Ownership After Death

Q. My brother and I worked together on his manuscript. He asked me to help rewrite, edit and type his work. When he passed away, all the manuscripts he had were packed into a box and given to me. I have found some I am sure will sell with some rewriting and corrections. I would like to submit these for publication using both our given names and the last name. What are my legal rights? Will it be necessary to ask permission from his other heirs, and would I have to share any profits with them? These papers were an outright gift.

A. If these manuscripts were willed to you, then they are your possession and you may try to get them published without asking the permission of the other heirs. If there is any doubt about the legality of this "gift," it would be best to consult an attorney.

Information on Libel

Q. For about a year I have been collecting material for a critique of a psychosomatic therapy and panacea of all that troubles man and the world. The head of this well-organized metaphysical school is known to sue for libel any who dare to criticize his teachings. Is there a school teaching writer protection rights?

A. We're not able to offer you expert legal advice. This can come only from a paid attorney. There are several books on libel which might prove helpful to you in your studies and you might want to look these up in the library. The book *Say it Safely* stresses the legal limits in publishing, radio and television.

Deductions

Q. I have a problem that probably is common to aspiring professional writers. Are there any publications that offer information regarding the writer and IRS? The reason for the question is simple; my 1967 return was audited and my expenses as a writer (second source of income) were questioned. Specifically, they exceeded the income I derived from that source. I was told that deductions would be allowed only for the amount of income, costs beyond that amount were not deductible.

A. It is not true that you can only deduct expenses equal to your income as a freelance writer. Writing is no different from any other business and certainly many businesses have expenses in some years exceeding their income and take a loss. This very fact was covered in an article we published in our April 1966 issue whose sub-head announced that you don't have to sell anything to deduct your expenses as long as you can prove you're seriously in the business of trying to make money from writing. All the articles on tax matters in *Writer's Digest* have been checked by the IRS in Washington, DC.

Using Real Names

Q. Is it *permissible,* in a book of personal experiences, to use real names and to relate real episodes, without obtaining written permission from the persons mentioned? Or, do you specifically recommend that both characters and events be fictionalized?

A. It's always advisable to change the names of real persons and the locale of real episodes, to avoid suits for invasion of privacy by the parties concerned. Even if your copy is nothing but complimentary, the individual sometimes resents being placed in the public spotlight and goes to court to prove his point.

Chapter 13

Preparing The Manuscript

Underline for Italics

Q. I am working on a short story in which short paragraphs in italics are interspersed throughout the narrative, and would like to know whether there is any way to indicate italics without underlining. This amounts to quite extensive underlining, which, in my opinion, is not only bothersome and time consuming but is distracting to the reader. A beginning writer cannot afford to distract an editor any more than he can help!

A. Underlining *is* the standard way to denote italics; editors would not be any more distracted by it than readers would be by the actual italics.

Children's Story Mss

Q. I would like to know if I am preparing my manuscripts of children's stories in the most favorable manner. I type them as I would any short story, without illustrations and without any suggestions or indications for same.

A. Yes, your presentation is acceptable. Leave the matter of illustration to the publisher who buys the story.

Which Type?

Q. I have only one typewriter and it has elite type. I know when manuscripts are submitted that pica is preferred. But does it make that much difference?
A. Relax, both pica and elite are acceptable. It's the more "exotic" types, such as fancy script or all capitals, that editors find objectionable.

Children's Books

Q. My husband and I are writing and illustrating a book for children. What media are used for children's book illustrations and how are the illustrations submitted?

A. One publisher of juvenile books suggests opaque water color (which comes in tubes) and the use of illustration board for best results. But just remember that if your book is accepted, the publisher will probably have his own ideas about how it should be illustrated, so I would prepare a few sample illustrations only, until you get an okay from a publisher.

Retype Again?

Q. Is it essential that a manuscript be neat? I have a 480 page ms. that I've retyped three times and it's still a mess. Every time I retype it, I reread it, which is disastrous because my pen flies with revisions, (usually of words, not sentences). If I retype it again, I'll be wasting weeks that could be used in creating. Or should I send it out with the "neat" word-substitutes.

A. Since you can't resist revising every time you retype, you would probably find a professional manuscript typist the answer to your problem. The cost of this service would be worth the considerable saving in time and effort. Under no circumstances should you send out a manuscript that has corrections marked on it, "neat" or not. Also to save wear and tear on the finished product, send the publisher a query letter first instead of submitting the complete manuscript.

Dot or Dashes

Q. Is there any current guide with editorial sanction for the use of the three . . .'s and the—? If so I would appreciate being let in on it.

A. There is no strict editorial policy governing the use of the three . . .'s and the—. In the popular magazines such as *McCall's, Esquire, Argosy, New Yorker* and *Redbook* the dash seems to be more prevalent than the dots, though most of the magazines do use both, sometimes in the same story. The dots are used mainly to indicate that the speaker's voice trails off . . .; the dash

is used sometimes in place of parentheses or sometimes to indicate an abrupt interruption in speech or thought or to suggest a pause longer than a comma but not as final as a period. The dots are also used to show omission of words from a quote; e.g., *Senator John L. McGee said "We must examine closely . . . the effect of postal rate increases on the magazine industry."* This statement could have appeared in a magazine industry newsletter where the omitted words *"agriculture grants, education prosposals, and,"* would have been of little interest to the readers of the newsletter.

Writing Mechanics

Q. I have often read the term "manuscript mechanics." Would you please tell me what this means?

A. This term refers to the business of making a manuscript as attractive as possible from the standpoint of overall appearance. It entails neatness of typing, punctuation, width of margins, centering of titles, etc.

Pen Name

Q. Could you tell me how one indicates on a manuscript that he is writing under a pseudonym?

A. Your real name should appear on the upper left-hand corner of each page of your manuscript. But if you're determined to keep your identity a secret from your readers, then on the title page, use your pseudonym in the byline. Of course, if you don't want even your editor or publisher to know your real name, then you'll have to be a little trickier and use the pseudonym in the byline, in the upper left-hand corner *and* on the return envelope. In this case, you'll have to notify your local post office of this name change.

Credits for Quotes

Q. Where should quotation credits be given in a manuscript—at the bottom of the page where it appears or at the end of the manuscript?

A. Usually credits are given by placing an asterisk next to the quote and a corresponding asterisk and notation of credits at the bottom of the page.

Testimonials

Q. Clifford Beers' book, *A Mind That Found Itself,* had many letters by famous people praising his work and book. I believe these letters were one of the factors that made his book such a success. Would you advise me to type an extra copy or two of the book I'm writing and send it to various people for similar letters to be printed in my book?

A. The garnering of letters of praise from famous people will usually be taken care of by the publisher's publicity department. Remember that you haven't yet obtained a contract for the book you're working on, so wait until the publisher accepts your ms before discussing testimonials with him.

Date Style

Q. In my writing, I often need to refer to the days and months of the year, omitting the year. It is correct, is it not, to use ordinal numerals to designate the days, for example: January 12th, May 1st, March 5th?

A. The accepted practice seems to be the designation of days as follows: January 12, May 1, March 5. For reference, see Winston Churchill's celebrated histories, *The Grand Alliance, The Gathering Storm,* etc.

Religious Ms

Q. Will you please tell me where I could send a religious manuscript to be read and edited? It is one my father wrote some ten years ago before his death in 1961. I found it some time ago and read it and feel it is good enough to be published. It is mimeographed and is single spaced (approximately 9,500 words). Would I have to retype this and double space it?

A. Yes, if you want your father's manuscript to have a proper reading at an editorial office, it will have to be retyped, double-spaced on 8½" by 11" paper. Since its length of 9,500 words is too long for an article in a magazine and too short for a book, I am at a loss to suggest a market to you for it. If when retyping it, you see how it might be cut and edited, then I would suggest you send it to an appropriate magazine. A list of religious magazines appears in the *Writer's Market.*

When To Hyphenate

Q. What is the fundamental rule, if there is one, about hyphenated words?

A. If you consult the introductory pages of most standard unabridged dictionaries, you will find rules pertaining to the use of hyphens. Rules *can* get to be rather complicated. But a few simples ones to bear in mind are that the hyphen can be used (1) to clarify meaning, e.g., honey-child ... not a child made of honey; (2) to avoid having a double vowel or a triple consonant, e.g., wall-like is preferable to walllike; (3) to aid proper pronunciation, e.g., all-embracing is less likely to be mispronounced than allembracing. In general, just remember that if the hyphen helps to make your meaning clearer, use it.

Novel Ms Preparation

Q. I am embarking on a novel and need to know the following: Is it single or double-spaced? Is there a margin to consider? Is the average novel from 60,000 to 80,000 words? Should I send a query or complete ms? Should I use bond paper?

A. Double-space your manuscript, leaving about a one-inch margin all around. Various publishers have different word requirements (see *Writer's Market* listings under "Book Publishers"), but many of the novels do fall into the 60-80,000 word group. Use standard 8½ × 11 typewriter bond paper. Instead of mailing the whole manuscript, first send out a synopsis plus two or three sample chapters and a letter asking if the publisher is interested. Be sure to include postage and an envelope for the return of your material.

Thoughts in Quotes?

Q. I have been told that thoughts should not be enclosed in quotation marks. This works very well in some cases, but there are instances in which I do not know how to handle the punctuation, as in the following: Jim said, "Walter is a wonderful fellow." Alice agreed and thought, "You are wonderful too." Should quotation marks be used in this case, and if not, should "You" begin with a capital letter?

A. Quotation marks need not be used here, but the capital letter for "You" should be retained. Or, if the use of a capital in the middle of a sentence disturbs you, you might handle it this way: Alice agreed. You are wonderful too, she thought. If you like, you may underscore her thought to indicate italics, which would differentiate it nicely from the direct quotations.

Quotation Credits

Q. I am writing a textbook. In places, for a line or so, I quote either from Webster's Dictionary or an encyclopedia; in others I use their material but reword it to make it simple for a child to understand. Will it be sufficient, at the end of the book, to give references used without listing each single place in which they are used?

A. You may safely reword the reference book material to make it understandable to children. And although it is usually necessary to request permission to quote from copyrighted material, in your case your quotations would undoubtedly come under the principles of "fair use" which legally allow *brief* quotations for scholarly purposes. Correct acknowledgement of the source material as you propose should be acceptable.

Triple Space?

Q. I triple space on manuscripts rather than double space because my typewriter has elite (small) type. Is this acceptable to magazine editors or do they always prefer double spacing?

A. Double spacing is preferable but I think triple spacing would be acceptable to magazine editors. You'll just have to try it out and see.

Manuscript Count

Q. I have never learned how writers arrive at the total number of words in a manuscript. Can you tell me?

A. Count every word on five representative pages; divide by 5 to get an average number of words per page and then multiply that average by the total number of pages in the manuscript. When counting words, abbreviated words count as one word as does the word "a," "the", etc.

How Long?

Q. Can you help me? I need to know how many words will make an average radio story of sixty minutes?

A. Radio feature copy usually runs fifteen double-spaced lines to equal one minute or about two pages to equal three minutes. The crux of the matter, of course, is how fast the narrator speaks. A thumbnail guide to the average length of other manuscript forms appeared in the article "How Long Is A. . . . ?" in August, '65 *Writer's Digest*.

Chapter 14

How To Sell What You Write

Better Market?

Q. I have written several hundred original epigrams and two and four line poetical proverbs which I believe are good. If they are acceptable to publishers, what would be most profitable to me, submit them in manuscript form for book publication, or in small lots to magazines that use this type of material?

A. Since it is usually easier for a beginner to sell to a magazine rather than a book publisher, it might be to your advantage to send these fillers to magazine markets. If possible, try to retain book rights so that eventually you can perhaps publish them as a collection in book form.

Writing and Selling Greeting Cards

Q. "What's Wrong With These Studio Card Ideas," in the October, 1968 issue is very interesting. Would you also be so kind as to give me some information on books or other material in which I can get a better idea of how to write greeting card ideas?

A. See *The Greeting Card Writer's Handbook,* edited by H. Joseph Chadwick, ($4.95) published by *Writer's Digest.*

True—But Not a Story

Q. After moving to this city, where the crime rate is unusually high, I've had several frightening narrow escapes. I would like to write about these but they would be short, with no exciting endings. In only one did I exchange words with my would-be attacker. Do you think some magazine would be interested or do you advise that I just forget it?

A. These first-person experiences could be written up as nonfiction articles but only if they would also offer some sound, constructive new insight into this problem and its solution. This would involve factual research with police departments, safety bureaus and other "experts." As an example of article style on a related subject, see the article "I'm Glad I Tried to Help!" in the April, 1965 issue of *Good Housekeeping.*

Comedy Skits

Q. Big Name Entertainers have Big Name Writers. But I think my material would be welcome to some little-known comedian. How is the best way to learn the names and addresses of such entertainers needing comedy routines when I live in an area where comedians seldom appear because the natives' chief amusement is listening to the cornstalks popping as they grow or watching pigs fight for a faucet at their mama's dinnerplace?

A. Provided that your Iowa corn remains in your fields and not in your jokes, several avenues are open to you. Since it's helpful to know a comedian's style of delivery, watch for rising young entertainers on the TV shows emceed by Merv Griffin, Mike Douglas and Johnny Carson and contact these newcomers in care of those programs. You might also treat yourself to a subscription to *Variety,* the show business newspaper that is sure to mention the names and places where lesser-known comedians appear. In fact, you might get this information from the newspapers of any large city. You could also place an ad in *Variety,* offering your material for sale.

Historical Sports?

Q. I write sports articles, mainly covering great football games of forty to fifty years ago but it is difficult to find magazines interested in them. I am wondering if editors think these are outdated and prefer something more modern.

A. Current sports magazines do seem to favor more contemporary subjects. Get in the habit of studying *Sport* and *Sports Illustrated* for a better idea of the type of material these magazines are looking for. While there may not be a current market for articles on great football *games* as such—is there a market for some of your material if you would do this: select a specific sports figure of these earlier days. Was he also a well-known businessman or prominent Lion or Rotarian later on? Perhaps there is a market among the fraternal magazines for such a piece. For some ideas on slanting magazine articles see the article "Don't Try to Sell Ice to Eskimos" in the November, 1968 *Writer's Digest.*

Greeting Card Idea

Q. I understand that greeting card companies purchase "ideas" as well as original verse. Would a suggestion that they use a poem by a well-known author come under the classification of an "idea"? The poem I have in mind was written in the 16th century so there would be no copyright problem.

A. Your suggestion could be considered an "idea" that you could try selling to some of the greeting card verse publishers listed in *Writer's Market.*

Textbook Publishers

Q. In the September 1968 issue of *Writer's Digest,* Anne McGravie discusses an exciting new freelance market, "Textbook Reader Stories." She suggests query letters to Textbook Publishers, but she does not suggest any that would be receptive to freelancers. It may be that Miss McGravie could not name any publishers, but it leaves the reader wondering where to start.

A. We listed a number of textbook publishers in the September '68 *Writer's Digest.* Check the contents page under "Markets" for the page number.

19 Markets For the Same Idea?

Q. I am puzzled by writers who claim that after mailing a piece out 19 times, and having it rejected, they mail it out once more and sell it. Are they telling the truth? It seems to me that if a piece is slanted to a given magazine and it's rejected, there are just not 19 other magazines with similar editorial policies where the piece could be offered.

A. These writers *are* telling the truth, because they have carefully explored all possible allied market areas. For instance, a piece about Washington State fishing may not sell to other specialized sports magazines, but it might find a place in some of that state's Sunday supplements or in general men's magazines, fraternal order publications, etc. The number of markets a writer finds depends on his own resourcefulness and ability to revise, where necessary, to suit the new market.

Photo Markets

Q. I am interested in a market for my photographs. I am currently stationed in Vietnam in the service of the U.S. Army. I am equipped with a Pentax 135MM camera plus numerous auxil-iary lenses and other photographic equipment. I work in psychological warfare and civic actions, and through my job and contacts with the local people I have the chance to take many interesting pictures. I would appreciate any information you might be able to provide me concerning sales of, or a chance to show my work.

A. There are hundreds of markets for the photographs you describe (either as single shots or a photo story) listed in the *Writer's Market,* under a variety of categories, but especially the wire services such as AP Newsfeatures, 50 Rockefeller Plaza, New York, N.Y. 10020 and United Press International, 220 E. 42nd St. New York, N.Y. 10017, listed in the "Syndicates" chapter.

Childrens' Series

Q. I have a new idea for a series of children's books. How would I sell this series to a publisher? What are my rights? What are the usual rates and how do I state them?

A. Query the publisher with an outline of the proposed series and some sample chapters. The questions of rights (such as Book Club, Reprints, etc.) and rates would usually be negotiated by the writer or his agent with the publisher upon acceptance of the work and receipt of his contract terms. The usual royalties on a juvenile are 7-15%, often split 50-50 with the illustrator. In some cases, the illustrator is paid a flat fee and the author receives full royalty.

Humor Book

Q. I have a book-length manuscript on wit and humor which is in the form of quips, jokes, doggerel, etc. What first step do you advise me to take?

A. You might try to sell the manuscript to a book publisher. In your local library or bookshop, find some humor books and then query their publishers. Also consult the list of Book Publishers in *Writer's Market*. You might be more successful in selling these items individually or in small batches. See the *Writer's Market* listings under the subhead, Fillers and under Cartoonists Wanting Gags.

Sell Article Twice?

Q. Is it unethical to cover similar material in different ways for different types of magazines (e.g., general and special education journal) or does an editor automatically assume that information in an article is offered to him exclusively?

A. It is common practice among non-fiction writers to get the most out of their research by slanting various aspects of their subject toward different markets. However, there has to be enough distinction between your treatment for the general markets and that for the education journal so that you cannot be accused of selling the same story to two magazines.

"Beginners' Markets"

Q. Do you have a listing of secondary markets where a 'neophyte' can break in?

A. Just because a magazine doesn't have a large circulation or pay much, doesn't mean its editor isn't just as demanding about the material it uses. In addition to the hundreds of smaller circulation and low pay publications listed in the annual editions of the *Writer's Market,* however, there will also be a group of these publications listed in the *1969 Writer's Yearbook.*

Cook Book Market?

Q. Is there any market for cookbooks from unknowns, menu planning and preparing meals for the working girls, or full-fledged dinner parties, etc., and how would one go about breaking into this field?

A. There has been such an influx of cookbooks on today's market that any new one would probably need a specialized approach that hasn't been tried before. See if you can gather together recipes that relate to an appealing, unusual central theme. Send a query letter, including a brief outline, to those book publishers, as listed in *Writer's Digest*, who are interested in cookbooks. For example, Doubleday & Co., Inc. (277 Park Ave., New York, N.Y. 10017), has a special Cookbook Department, to which such material should be sent.

Comedy Skits

Q. I've written several short comedy skits. Could you tell me where to submit them, and how to go about it?

A. Much would depend on the subject matter and the level of humor that is employed. There are various possible markets such as radio, TV, school productions, etc. If you think your skits could be used on television, for example, you would have to submit them to specific TV entertainers through an agent. If the skits could be considered one-act plays suitable for school productions, you could send them to play publishers who specialize in this area, such as The Heuer Publishing Company, etc. See the *Writer's Market* under "Play Publishers".

Truth or Fiction?

Q. In general, is a story more salable if the publisher can present it as a true story rather than the same story fictionalized?

A. This depends on whether the publisher is in the market for fiction or nonfiction. If he generally buys both, then the writer must decide which category best suits his subject. There would not be any particular preference for a true story over a fictional one . . . just a good one!

Heroes for Sale

Q. "Write on familiar subjects," the novice is advised. I have written about real flesh-and-blood people, whose traits of character were admirable, and who I felt were making noteworthy contributions to society. But where is there a market for such articles?

A. Many newspapers, such as the *Cincinnati Enquirer,* run such profiles of interesting members of the community. Perhaps you could interest your local newspaper editor in the idea. There is also the possibility that these people you write about, work for companies that publish House Organs which could use such material. Then, too, their "contributions to society" might also suggest other specialized markets. (See *Writer's Market* listings.)

Family Adventure

Q. I sincerely believe that my family and I have had more unusual incidents in our lives than most people, and I would like to gather these happenings, both funny and tragic, together in a story in the third person, changing all the names and places. Am undecided whether to start from my childhood or when I was about to enter the business world, using some anecdotes from my younger years in flashbacks. Would there be a market for a book of that type?

A. Family adventure stories have been popular for a long time (e.g. *Swiss Family Robinson, Cheaper by the Dozen,* etc.). There might be a market for yours too, but only if the story is exceptionally well written and offers incidents that have strong, universal appeal for the reader. Consider starting the story at a point of high interest in the leading character's life, and use flashbacks sparingly.

Market for Illustrations?

Q. I wonder if your office would be so kind as to oblige me with the names and addresses of advertising concerns who might be in the market for illustrations for advertising purposes.

A. Most advertising agencies have their own staffs of artists. However, if you are interested in doing work for local art agencies, I suggest you consult the Yellow Pages of your Telephone Directory, under the heading, "Artists," where you will find a list of agencies that do commercial advertising art. You may also try writing to: American Association of Advertising Agencies, 200 Park Ave., New York, N.Y. or to American Advertising Federation, 655 Madison Ave., New York, N.Y. 10021

Series Humor?

Q. Was interested to read in May, '66 WD that United Features Syndicate accepts fact articles to be published in series form. Is there such an outlet for a series of "humorous commentaries" on the condition of modern life? Would it be best to write to a magazine? Is it better to submit articles individually?

A. Try querying those Syndicates listed in *Writer's Market* that best seem to suit your needs. However, it might be less difficult to place these humorous essays individually in magazines.

Syndicating a Column

Q. Somewhere I read that it is permissible to send samples of a suggested syndicate column to several syndicates at the same time. Is this information correct?

A. No, the sample columns should be sent to only one syndicate at a time. However, perhaps you are thinking of syndicating your own column. In that case you would send your sample columns simultaneously to the various in-

dividual newspaper editors (in noncompeting circulation areas, of course) you think might be interested in buying such a feature.

Book Rights

Q. I'd like to write a number of articles in the form of letters about a street I've lived on for 17 years. If these letters were acceptable to a syndicate, suppose I later might want them put in a book. How would I present them to a syndicate with such a thought in mind—regarding later use?

A. Simply specify that you wish to retain book rights.

Get an Assignment

Q. I have a professional paper which has a number of takers in the field for which I have written, but they all say they do not pay except for material written on assignment. A friend told me, "Get the assignment." How do I get an assignment to do a paper that is already done?

A. Assignments are the result of an editor's need to have a certain topic covered in print. Because he urgently wants such an article, he is willing to pay for it. He usually gives assignments only to established writers whose work he is familiar with and whom he knows he can rely on. Have you tried to find a publication in your particular field which *does* pay for free-lance material? Check *Writer's Market* for payment rates. If you find that all the likely prospects are nonpaying, except on assignment, then choose one to whom you have not previously submitted your paper. Write this editor a lively, interesting query which will convince him of the need for such an article. Request that, if the editor deems the idea worthy of publication, you be given the assignment. Remember that since you are a stranger to him, you should show why you should be given the assignment. Include some pertinent autobiographical facts that clearly qualify you to write with authority on this subject. You might even provide a sample paragraph to give him an idea of the style, treatment, etc., you would use.

British Fiction

Q. In a recent letter from a writer friend I am told that editors of magazines in Great Britain are receptive toward fiction in which the locale is in our early West and Southwest. Can you give me the names and addresses of magazines that are published in Great Britain, particularly those which publish fiction? Also, what are the postage rates and how about return postage?

A. You'll find the information you want in *Writers and Artists Yearbook* which lists a great variety of magazines published in England, Scotland, Australia, Ireland, etc. Consult your local post office about purchasing International Postal Exchange Coupons for mailing material overseas.

The Comic Book Market

Q. Could you tell me if comic books buy freelance material? What are the usual rates? The usual lengths? Is the story sent in regular manuscript form or is there a special form? Are there any books on the subject?

A. Different comic book publishers have different policies concerning the purchase of material. The juvenile magazine, *Treasure Chest,* for example, will consider freelance stories. Their present rate is $10.00 per published page, and they recommend the submission of story ideas or synopses for approval. They do prefer a special form, and if you will write to them, in care of George A. Pflaum, Publisher, Inc., 38 W. Fifth St., Dayton, Ohio 45402 they will send you an example you may follow. A story for them may be six pages or less. Dell Publishing Company (750 Third Avenue, New York, N.Y. 10017) buys some freelance material for its comic books, but this material is written on assignment. The editorial staff determines the current needs and then assigns a story to a writer and designates its length. Mr. Don Arneson, Editor of Dell Comics, offers this helpful advice to would-be comic book writers: "Actual scripting of a comic book is a bit different from other types of writing in that the medium is primarily a visual one. Movie scripting is perhaps the closest parallel. The writer of a comic must 'see' his action first, then fill in the visual gaps with verbal continuity. The greatest error, in my estimation, is redundancy in dialogue or caption and illustration. To picture the hero as he crashes his fist into his antagonist's jaw and then place in caption, "The hero crashes his fist into . . etc." becomes a waste of effort. With only 32 pages to tell a story, each bit of space must be utilized to the fullest. Also, complete verbal description of a thing, a person or what-have-you is ill-spent effort, for the illustration can do this better. Unlike prose, comics stimulate the imagination both graphically and verbally. The idea is to move the reader in and out of the picture you have drawn, not to have the reader create his own pictures." Two books that might prove useful are: *Comics and Their Creators* (1942) by Sheridan Martin and *The Comics* (1947) by Coulton Waugh. See also Jack Markow's column, "The Comic Strippers" in the August 1963 issue of *Writer's Digest*. A more recent book is *These Top Cartoonists Tell How They Create America's Favorite Comics* (1964) by Allen Willette.

Stories on Record

Q. For about a year, I had a program on a local station where I worked without scripts, just from notes. One day each week I devoted to children's stories, part fantasy but most important, many facts concerning the particular fishes involved. It seems to me this would be a painless way of introducing youngsters to the fascination of marine biology. Is there a potential market for material of this type? I have it all on tapes, and am afraid I do not have the attentiveness to detail and composition necessary to a good writer.

A. Why not try querying some of the record companies that put out children's records? Be sure to mention your radio program.

Prize Winning Poem Marketable?

Q. May a poem later be offered for sale to a magazine if it was entered in a prize contest and read over the radio or if it received a prize or if it was circulated in a mimeographed brochure that carried notice that the author retains all rights?

A. Yes, such a poem may be submitted to professional markets, but some indication of its previous exposure could be included.

Newspaper Column Syndication

Q. How do you market material for a daily or weekly newspaper column, a women's page feature, to a syndicate? When readers' comments, which are welcomed, are integrated into the column, do you need the readers' permission before printing their comments or names? How do you protect your idea and your rights? How do you determine a rate and how do you state it when submitting samples? Are there syndicates that purchase fillers? If so, how do you submit them?

A. Write a query letter to the editor of the syndicate that best suits your needs, and if you wish, enclose a sample column, and be sure to include a stamped, self-addressed envelope. Ideas cannot be copyrighted, but once the material is published, it can secure copyright protection. The unpublished columns are protected by common law copyright. If the column clearly invites readers to submit their comments for publication, then there is no need to request permission to quote. The rate of payment is usually fixed by the syndicate, not by the writer. It may be anywhere from 40 to 60% of the gross proceeds; however, there are some syndicates that pay the writer a salary or a minimum guarantee. There are syndicates that buy fillers. The fillers should be typed individually on separate sheets of paper. If you are not familiar with the various types of syndicates, consult *Writer's Market* which provides a detailed account of each syndicate's rate of payment and field of specialization.

Shopping Guide

Q. I've succeeded in interesting three local grocers here in a weekly combination hand-bill and news-sheet which I shall have mimeographed. If my grocer-sponsors agree, is there any reason why I can't legally accept *paid* ads from other non-competitive local businesses? Also, my grocer-sponsors will be paying me for these sheets but they will be offered *free* to patrons. Can I legally "lift" quotes from published material without bothering to get permission from author or publisher?

A. It would be permissible to accept paid ads, provided your grocer-sponsors have no objections. Regardless of whether or not your publication is of-

fered free, however, you *should* get permission from the copyright owners to quote from published material, if it is of any length. Brief quotes, are permissible without writing in advance under the "fair use" provision of the Copyright Law.

Film Market for Animal Stories?

Q. I am a professional story teller via radio. I write my own children's stories and songs. My animal stories would lend themselves to film cartoons. Will you please advise me if there is an open market for this?

A. Most film companies work through agents or on the basis of assignment. You might write a West Coast agent (see list in *Writer's Market*) about your radio credits and try to get his representation for your idea with a film company.

Publishing Poems

Q. Is it wise to let a small "little magazine" use poetry to get it into print or "hold out" for better markets? If winning any contest prizes, does one retain the right to sell same work?

A. "Holding out" can be a frustrating game. There is a prestige and satisfaction in being published by the "little magazines," so don't be afraid to try them—if they are copyrighted. If they are not, your poem's publication will place it in the public domain and you will have to write a new version to obtain a copyright if you wanted to, say, incorporate it in a book of poems later. Usually contests permit the contestant to retain all rights to his work, but it is best to check the rules in each case.

Fictional Confession?

Q. May a confession story be entirely fictional? If so, would it be best to sign such a story simply "By Pen-name" even when the heroine's (fictional) name is a different one and the story is told in first person?

A. The important thing about a confession story is that it *could* happen, not that it did, so it's all right for it to be fictional. Since confessions do not give bylines, it is unnecessary to be concerned about pen-names for them. Only the editors know who the authors are . . . and they don't tell the readers!

Downbeat Story Market?

Q. I have written a story about a woman's emotional disintegration as various pressures upon her pass that point where she can no longer cope with them. It does not end happily. A recent editorial comment said, ". . . it's a little too grim to be entirely satisfactory to us." I believe this attitude toward an unhappy ending is shared by all the women's magazines. And this is definitely a woman's story; it is *not* a Confession. I am discouraged, not by rejections per se, but by the apparent lack of markets for this kind of story. Are there any suggestions in your excellent bag of tricks?

A. If the calibre of your writing is high, you could try the quality markets, such as *Atlantic, Harper's,* etc. However, please bear in mind that your story must have something to say to readers above and beyond the mere chronicling of one woman's misfortunes. It must in some way deepen readers' insight through its larger view of life.

Book Reviewing

Q. About book reviewing—How does one go about breaking into this field? I have worked in the Public Library and I also have sold a few of my juvenile stories.

A. Try submitting a book review to your local newspaper or to some of the smaller magazines (religious or women's) that do print reviews. Inform them of your sales in the juvenile field and ask them if they would like to use your services. (**Ed. Note.** Writers are reminded most local newspapers and small magazines do not pay for reviews except with the book itself.)

Foreign Markets

Q. Is it true that foreign publishers disdain the cover letters that so many American writers enclose with their manuscripts?

A. I am not aware of any foreign aversion to cover letters unless it is to the over-long, redundant or "chatty" type of letter that U.S. publishers would be hostile to also.

Juvenile Book Reprint?

Q. Would it be possible for me to have my juvenile book, now out of print, published as a reprint edition? If so, which publishers could I contact regarding same?

A. You might query publishers of reprints in the juvenile field, such as Berkeley Publishing Corporation, 200 Madison Ave. New York, N.Y. 10016. For additional listings, please consult the latest edition of *Writer's Market*.

Children's Sayings

Q. Do you know any magazine which would be interested in some very funny sayings of children which I have collected from children I have known?

A. For submission of individual funny sayings, try *Reader's Digest*. If you could incorporate these sayings into a humorous feature article, this might be material for women's magazines such as *McCall's, Good Housekeeping, etc.*

Advertising Slogans

Q. Can you offer any suggestions as to how to sell *original* mottoes, slogans, etc. for advertising?

A. Selling original mottoes, slogans, etc., for advertising is a very difficult thing since many national advertisers automatically reject any idea submissions of this type from individuals because they are afraid of plagiarism suits. A few freelancers have been successful in placing advertising slogans with local advertising agencies who are handling a local client's work. For your nationally distributed product slogan ideas consult the Standard Directory of Advertisers. Companies are listed in this book by products. By selecting a company you could then find from the listing which advertising agency is currently handling their account. Then you could write the advertising agency to find out whether or not they would be willing to look at your idea and if usable, pay you for it

Special Market

Q. Do you know if any manufacturer of aluminum publishes a magazine that might be interested in freelance work connected with the aluminum industry?

A. The American Metal Market Company, 525 West 42nd Street, New York, N.Y., 10036 publishes a house organ, *Metal/Center News,* and a trade journal, *American Metal Market,* which deal with aspects of the aluminum industry. For additional information please see *Writer's Market*.

Sell Ideas?

Q. Is there a market for ideas for scripts and stories and possibly films? I have several ideas for science fiction pieces but feel that I am not in a position to expand them into saleable pieces.

A. All television and picture producers and magazine editors will look at completed scripts, not simply ideas. In addition television producers require that material be submitted through agents and will not look at material submitted directly. Perhaps you have a friend who is a good writer, but short on ideas, with whom you could collaborate.

Church-School Papers

Q. I am interested in doing some writing for church-school papers and magazines. Where can I find lists of these markets?

A. The *Writer's Market,* ($7.95, published by *Writer's Digest*) lists hundreds of religious markets along with many other types of magazines, book publishers and other firms seeking material from freelance writers. In addition, *Writer's Digest,* of course, carries various market listings each month in an effort to cover all of the creative fields throughout the year.

Submitting Strip Ideas

Q. In collaboration with a local commercial artist, I am developing an idea for a daily paper comic strip. We hope to have some material to offer soon. Could you send me information concerning the size of drawings, the number of episodes which should be submitted, and other requirements made by syndicates to whom we expect to submit our work?

A. In the exclusive interview in the *1967 Writer's Yearbook* Milton Caniff, creator of *Steve Canyon,* suggested 12 to 18 daily strips, entirely finished. For

Sunday strips—at least two. One Sunday sample should be reduced to newspaper size by means of a matte photo print and hand colored to simulate the finished product as it would appear in the paper. (Caniff prefers to do his strip originals in a 6-7/8" x 21-5/8" size for the dailies and 17" x 23-1/8" for the Sunday strip.)

Special Background?

Q. Does one have to be an Editor, or need special training in order to write book reviews? I have often felt, after reading a book that I could write concise descriptive and honest opinions.

A. No, one does not need special training in order to write book reviews. If you can write interesting, brief reviews of a book that an editor wants to publish, that's all that matters. When contacting book review editors to see if they could use your work, the best thing to do would be to enclose a sample book review you have written on a relatively new book that you already own.

Sell TV Commercials?

Q. I often get popping ideas for various commercials, but how can I go about getting a start in this field? Can commercials be written freelance, or does each company hire their own staff of writers?

A. Yes, most companies have their own advertising departments as well as advertising agencies to prepare their commercials. It is, therefore, very difficult for a freelancer to submit material and have it accepted. The few writers who have been successful in this way have concentrated on companies and products in their immediate area, calling on the advertising manager of the company itself to present the idea.

When to Submit?

Q. Can you give me any general information about the time for submitting stories to quarterly publications or must this be secured for the individual publications? At the moment I am interested in submitting a Christmas story to a religious magazine which is a quarterly.

A. A Christmas story for a quarterly publication should be submitted at least six months in advance, but it would be best to query the individual editor yourself. as you suggested.

Jokes for Sale

Q. Where could I find markets for Jokes?

A. The markets for jokes are several: one, magazines, two, disc jockeys on radio stations, three, comedians who work in night clubs and on television. The magazine joke markets are all listed in our annual directory, the *Writer's Market*. Gags for disc jockeys can be submitted to them directly with a self-enclosed envelope for return. Jokes submitted to night club comics are usually submitted to them in care of the club where they are performing. Tele-

vision comedians depend almost entirely on staff writers and there is not much of a freelance market for jokes there.

Agent for Poetry?

Q. I am a poet who needs a literary agent. I wonder if you could help me find a reputable one who would work with me on agreeable terms.

A. There is such a small market today for poetry in books, that I don't know of a single agent who will handle someone whose sole output is poetry. Most poets attempt to sell their poems individually to magazines, hoping eventually to be able to present enough published credits to a book publisher to interest him in putting out an anthology of their work. If by literary agent you really meant literary critic, and would like to have an evaluation of your poetry by a professional, several firms, including *Writer's Digest* offer this service for a fee.

Selling a Column

Q. What can you suggest to read that would help in becoming a columnist—a chatty one, nothing serious. I have written several articles, but I don't know whether to take them to a local editor or not. I don't know how to prepare them.

A. You might want to refer to a book we publish called *The Creative Writer*, which has a comprehensive chapter devoted to "How to Syndicate Your Own

'Column." The experiences of several writers who did this were also described in the January, 1965, July '67 and August '68 issues of *Writer's Digest*.

Editorial Market?

Q. I am particulary interested in writing editorials. Any information will be appreciated.

A. Unfortunately, there isn't much of a market for editorials since most newspapers have their own staff writers who prepare the editorial page. The only thing you could do would be to contact newspaper editors in your immediate area—send along a few sample editorials, and try your luck.

Puzzle Markets

Q. I would like some information regarding the marketing of crossword puzzles. I have made a few which are now in varying stages of completion. I assume payment for crossword puzzles varies with the size of the puzzle. All mine are 15x15, though I do have a few 21x21. I have written four syndicates concerning crossword puzzles; one syndicate said they were well-stocked, thanks anyway; another said they did not use crossword puzzles and the other two didn't even have the courtesy to answer my letter.

A. Those magazines which buy puzzles are listed in our annual directory, *Writer's Market*. Magazines which do use puzzles usually want them aimed toward their specific audience, so it's usually a matter of creating a puzzle to fit a specific magazine rather than creating some puzzles and then trying to sell them. There are, of course, crossword puzzle magazines themselves and their names and addresses are also listed in the *Writer's Market*.

Humor For Sale

Q. We have written some material which we feel is humorous. We are interested in finding a market for this material, which is written in the form of comic dialogue. If you could send us any information which would be helpful, we would appreciate it. We are particularly interested in finding an agent who could market it for us.

A. I don't know of any agent who is interested in handling humorous material unless the writers have already attained a certain amount of success on their own. Most beginning comedy writers try to write specific comedy material for either night club comedians in their area or speakers at club gatherings, etc.

Translating Books?

Q. How does a beginner go about finding a book to translate? I have done numerous short translations (English to Spanish, and Spanish to English) but mostly business material, and one or two movie documentaries of about 10 minute duration. You constantly read of new books coming out translated by —now how can you get this type of work? Whom do you write to? Do they send you sample chapters to translate? What do you offer them as references if you have none. Although I have done many translations they have usually been for people passing through Spain —students, professors, here for a few months. I wouldn't know where to reach them for references, and they are not that well known.

A. American publishers who have published translations from Spanish literature are listed in the *Subject Guide to Books in Print* under, for example "Spanish Fiction—Translations From".

I suggest you write each of them and enclose a sample of your work and a description of the work you have done for professors even though you can't give their specific current addresses as reference. For additional advice on this subject you might want to write to the American Translators Association, Box 489 Madison Square Station, New York, N.Y. 10010.

Markets for Speeches?

Q. Someplace,—I thought it was in the *Writer's Digest,*—I saw a request for someone to do research for other writers, and to write speeches for women's clubs etc. Could you steer me in the right direction to locate and obtain such a job?

A. The only market like this *Writer's Digest* has published recently appeared in the February 1968 issue. Unfortunately Mr. Westreich has obtained all the material he needs at the present

time. As far as writing speeches for women's clubs is concerned,—if a specific woman who is an officer of a club requires a speech to be written for her, you would have to find this out on a local level, of course, and make your contact and sell your services directly. The same would hold true for local businessmen or politicians who need speech writers.

Easiest? Best? It Depends

Q. Who or what is the best market? Or most easily salable, for that matter?

A. There is no such thing as one best market since so much depends on the type of writing each individual writer does. A market is good for a particular writer if he writes the kind of material that market needs. In general there are more markets for articles than short stories.

Film Scripts

Q. In writing for film production companies, am I correct in thinking they are the ones who do the actual filming, not the script writer? Are scripts prepared like TV scripts?

A. Yes, the film production companies do the actual filming. Yes, the scripts are prepared like TV scripts. These film production companies, however, are not preparing films for exhibition in regular movie theaters as you probably know. Their films are "nontheatrical" and are specifically designed for industrial public relations use, sales training aids, etc. (Since the edition of *Writer's Market* containing this list is three years old, be prepared for some address changes. This particular category is not included in the '69 *Writer's Market*.)

Monologues for Children

Q. Could you please list the names and addresses of a few editors who would be interested in monologues for children?

A. The only publishers I know who buy monologues for children are the religious houses who put out Sunday school materials. They're listed in the "Juvenile and Young Peoples Magazines" category of the *Writer's Market*.

Recommend an Agent

Q. I would like to have you recommend an agent in the N.Y. Area. I am going to be 73 years old next November. My greatest ambition in life is to have this book published. I don't feel that I have the energy to trot around to publishing offices. I am too old.

A. All of the agents listed in our annual directory, *Writer's Market,* are thoroughly reputable and we would recommend any of them. Many agents, of course, are not willing to work with previously unpublished writers so you may have to write a number of them before you are able to find one that is interested in handling your work strictly on a commission basis. Why not try marketing your book yourself?—I don't mean taking it around personally to

publishers' offices—they hate that—and can't possibly give you an on-the-spot answer. Mail it to the publisher of your choice, always being sure to enclose sufficient return postage.

Humorous Monologues

Q. Who buys Humorous Monologues?

A. It depends on what the subject matter is and who the potential audience is. If, for example, your material is the type a night club comic could use in his routine—he's your market. If it's light, frothy material of the type that would appeal to a women's club—they're your market. A monologue implies a spoken delivery so there isn't any written, published market for this type of material. If by humorous monologue you really mean short prose humor—these markets are scattered throughout our annual directory, the *Writer's Market.*

Agent?

Q. Walt Disney Productions states that they look at original scripts only if submitted by an accredited agent. They list no agent's name, so how do I go about finding their agents? Could you give me this information? I have several children's stories, two of which would make excellent Cartoon Movies. Would the same agent handle both types of stories? I have sold poems, and had several more printed in free publications. And was told by several teaching friends that I did quality writing.

They have urged me to do something with my work, but I lack the push or the know how, I guess, for the business part of my work. Does the agent take care of all that? I have heard that an agent sometimes asks for a fee in advance. If this is true, how much is the accepted fee, and what is his total fee? Is it percentage of sales?

A. A list of agents with details on the types of material they handle appears in our annual directory, the *Writer's Market*. The agent tries to market your work and handles the business arrangement. You have to provide him with stories that he can sell of course. Some agents do not charge a reading fee, but they usually will not work with previously unpublished or unproduced writers. Other agents do charge reading fees and their fees are listed in the information we publish about them in our directory.

Sell Poems?

Q. I was wondering if you could help me get my poems published in magazines or something of that sort that usually pay a few dollars for poems and stories? I do believe that getting a book published is out of the question.

A. Yes, you are quite right, it is almost impossible these days to get a book of poems published unless you are an extremely well known and nationally recognized poet. There are a great many magazine markets for poetry, however, and they are all included in our annual directory, *Writer's Market*.

How to Sell Songs

Q. How does one go about getting his lyrics set to music and subsequently publishing a song?

A. The publishing of songs has changed so completely in recent years that it is almost impossible to do it by mail. The writer has to be on the scene in New York, Los Angeles, or Nashville and contact the artists and repertoire representatives of the individual record companies since they are the ones to whom songs are sold originally these days rather than to music publishers.

Chapter 15

More Writers' Questions

Talent or Therapy?

Q. I write a great deal in times of extreme despair, sorrow or stress. Might there be some indication of writing ability or is this merely a form of comfort or therapy instead of alcohol, ungovernable temper, over-eating or other?

A. A need to write does not necessarily denote an indication of ability or talent. It is not the motivation but the end result that counts. However, it is true that the channelling of tortured emotions into acts of creativity has sometimes been responsible for great works, such as the paintings of Van Gogh, the poetry of Keats.

Style

Q. Can you please tell me why some magazines appear to have all been written by the same author? Some are so much that way that even the articles are in exactly the same style as the fiction. Can any of these magazines that look to be all written by one person be considered free-lance markets?

A. The stories and articles in certain magazines may seem to be the product of one prolific writer, but you can rest assured that they're usually not. What happens is that each magazine has a certain style peculiar to itself. In the hope of selling to this market, many writers are careful to slant to the known preferences here. Then, of course, the editors may do a certain degree of rewrite, where the material warrants it, and this too would tend to give an additional familiar touch to the work. These magazines are considered free-lance markets.

Role Playing

Q. The question has often occurred to me as to whether a man can write effectively about a woman, or vice versa. If he is writing from the viewpoint of the woman or girl, could he possibly portray her problem and her various reactions to situations? Would he be better advised to choose a man as protagonist, or does it matter? What is the practice among successful writers?

A. There is enough proof in the literature of the world that a writer can successfully portray a member of the opposite sex. Look at what Shakespeare did with Cleopatra, what Flaubert did with Madame Bovary, and don't forget what Margaret Mitchell did with Rhett Butler, to name just a few. The ease with which a male writer can slip into the consciousness of a female character and vice versa depends ultimately on the individual writer and how much insight he has into the workings of human nature, regardless of sex.

Write? Don't??

Q. In the August '65 *Writer's Digest,* one famous writer's (Herbert Gold) advice to young writers is: "Don't write." In the same issue, Nancy Vogel says, "To be a writer you must write." What's your reaction on these opposite assertions?

A. These two statements, taken out of context, are not as contradictory as they may appear. Mr. Gold meant that instead of spending *all* his time writing, the young writer should expose himself to experience, involving himself in life so that he will, in time, have something to write about. In Miss Vogel's article, she was quoting Louis L'amour's advice which emphasized the need for a writer to discipline himself in order to avoid all those little excuses he invents to save him from actually sitting down and writing, e.g., sharpening pencils, changing typewriter ribbons, etc. The as-

sumption is, of course, that he has something to say and just needs to make himself get started.

First Readers

Q. In your March '63 "Help!" column you were asked about "a first reader" and you replied, "Through *her* experience and training *she* is able . . ." etc. Why not the generic "he?" Are all First Readers women? If so, why? Is it because they work for less?

A. Most First Readers do happen to be women. Maybe it's because they have more "patience and fortitude" than the "stronger" sex!

Dictating a Novel

Q. Since I am now going to tape-record the second draft of a novel, I would appreciate your informing me about (1) the fastest talking pace with which I can expect a good typist to get everything down on paper, and later, to proofread the tape; (2) the best words, or rather the exact wording to put to the tape-recorder to indicate: all punctuation, parentheses, italics, use of white spacing, etc.

A. Record at your own pace. The typist will adjust her speed accordingly. A good typist should be able to punctuate correctly from the way in which the lines are spoken. You will, however, have to indicate parentheses by saying, "Open parentheses" . . . and then later "Close parentheses." Say "Underline" when you want italics, and say "Paragraph" whenever you want to start a new paragraph. Before you begin, you can explain that you want double spacing except where you indicate otherwise.

Writers' Conference

Q. Do you know of any writers' conferences in the U.S. during November?

A. Sorry, I don't know of any writers' conference held in November but for future reference, each year in our May issue we publish a list of writers' conferences for that year.

A Writing Career

Q. Do you help new writers get their start in the business world? I want to have a career in writing but I find it difficult getting started.

A. A helpful booklet called *Jobs and Opportunities for Writers* has been published by the editors of *Writer's Digest* detailing the educational background, personality traits, and other requirements necessary for persons seeking certain types of staff writing jobs. The booklet also describes the average salaries paid and other details on each job.

Writers' Advocate

Q. Who is the patron saint of writers? Can you tell me something about him?

A. The patron saint of authors and journalists is St. Francis de Sales (1567-1622), Savoyard noble, Bishop of Geneva, Doctor of the Church. He preached that everyone, however busy, could have a spiritual life. He authored two masterpieces of religious writing: *Introduction To The Devout Life* and *Treatise On The Love Of God*. The ideas expressed in his works were instrumental in developing the Roman Catholic emphasis on loving God as well as fearing Him as a judge. His Feast Day is January 29 and two of his oft-quoted sayings are: "You can catch more flies with a spoonful of honey than with a hundred barrels of vinegar" and "What is good makes no noise. What is noisy does no good." And in case you're wondering, the patron saint of poets is St. David, of psalmist fame.

Writers Colonies

Q. I have read so much about the days in Paris when writers collected at certain addresses. Are there such places, where writers are known to collect informally today . . . Paris, London, New York City, Chicago, or other cities in the world? How can I find out the streets or addresses of such places?

A. No, there aren't any places in Paris, London, New York, Chicago or other major cities where writers are known to consistently gather, the way they did at the Ritz Bar in Paris and in certain cafes on the Left Bank. The MacDowell Colony in Peterborough, New Hampshire often has a few writers temporarily in residence along with artists and musicians, and occasionally on certain university campuses several will happen to appear at the same time, but this is coincidental.

Chapter 16

Motion Picture Scripts

Movie Musical

Q. When writing a screenplay musical, is it necessary to collaborate with a composer or songwriter; or may one simply make insertions in the play where a song should enter, describing what flavor the song should have?

A. Since motion picture producers have their own ideas about who should write the songs which might go in a musical, yes your best bet would be to simply make insertions in the play where the song should enter, describing the type of song you have in mind. Remember—most motion picture producers will not look at scripts submitted directly by writers, but they must be submitted through literary agents.

Movie Scripts

Q. I am writing a moving picture play and need to learn more about the camera shots. What I want is for some one familiar with movie writing to take parts of my play and set them to the proper shots.

A. Why don't you simply write up your story in standard script form and submit it to an accredited agent? Movie companies don't expect the material they buy to be worked out down to the smallest detail. Once your script is sold, the shots would become largely the concern of the director who will have a more practiced and knowing eye in this matter than you have.

Autobiography—Film

Q. I am writing a story about myself and my early life. I believe my story told in the right way would make an interesting movie. How can I get it into the hands of the right producer? I am writing it in play form. Is this acceptable and where would I send it to get it possibly made into a motion picture?

A. The play form is acceptable, but motion picture producers and studios will look at original scripts only if they are submitted through recognized agents. *Writer's Market* provides a current list of agents.

Chapter 17

Creating The Novel

Technical Accuracy?

Q. In writing a novel concerning the life of a professional person, such as a laboratory technician, would the author need official verification of the accuracy of technical matter in it before a book publisher would publish it, assuming the rest of the book was of publishable quality?

A. In a cover letter, it might be helpful to state the sources on which the technical information is based. If the publisher is interested and requires further substantiation, he will let you know.

Switch Viewpoint?

Q. In writing a novel using the Major Character viewpoint, is it permissible to switch—from chapter to chapter—from the third person to the first (and vice versa) or would this be too disturbing to the reader?

A. This switching of viewpoints from one character to another is permissible, but it would probably be less distracting to readers if all the viewpoints were in the third person.

Reader Identification

Q. I am considering a novel about a ballerina—a fourteen-year-old girl—and she is telling the story. I am concerned about Reader Identification. Will *adult* readers "identify" with a leading character of this age?

A. Adult readers *have* been known to identify with younger heroes and heroines. Shakespeare's Juliet was only about fourteen. However, since there is presently a strong need for books geared to teen-age interests, you might be wise to develop your story as juvenile fiction. With teen-age girls making up most of your readers, you should have no worries about their identification with your young ballerina.

Novel Manuscript

Q. I have just finished writing a novel, and I have a couple of problems. Could you tell me what the margins should be on a manuscript?

A. The margins on the left and right sides, the top and the bottom should each be about one inch.

Author's Name

Q. Does the name of the writer of a book-length manuscript have to appear on every page of the manuscript? I was under the impression that the writer's name and address were only necessary on the title page. I have two book-length manuscripts about finished now, and was wondering about that. At the present time I have only the chapter number and the chapter page on every page after the title page. If the name is to appear on the upper left hand corner of the page, then should the manuscript title appear on every page along with the chapter number and page number?

A. The recommended form includes the author's name in the upper left-hand corner of each page and the page number in the upper right hand corner. The appearance of the author's name on every page is simply a form of protection for you and a help to the editor in case some pages inadvertently get separated from the rest during reading and handling. Most publishers, incidentally, prefer pages to be numbered consecutively—not by page number within each chapter.

Copyright

Q. How important is it for a new writer, or any writer for that matter, to secure a copyright for his book manuscript before submitting it to the trade houses for publication or consideration? Isn't it safe to entrust this somewhat bothersome detail to the publisher when and if publication is insured?

A. There are two types of copyright. One, known as "common law" copyright, automatically protects orginal work prior to publication. The other type of copyright is the more familiar, "statutory" copyright which must be obtained upon publication and public dissemination of the work. The publisher who buys the manuscript usually does take care of these copyright details, and it is spelled out in the contract you sign.

The Rules?

Q. I am doing research for a proposed biographical novel, my first of this type. My famous people on whom I am basing my novel lived in the early 1800's. Naturally I am not always able to get to an original letter or document written by the subject, and so I am taking much of this from factual books of other writers in which they quote from these originals. . . . Can you tell me please the rules about biographical novels? Must I get permission from all of these authors I have read in order to put certain words in my character's lips which obviously he has said? Must I get permission from whoever might have the original letters or manuscripts or documents ... if I can find whoever has them? And how about a book that was written in this 1800 period by the famed person himself ... may I use this material in building up my character? What about any living descendants of these famed people ... could they object?

A. In a novel of this type, you could acknowledge, in an Introduction or Preface, the sources on which the factual material is based. Write to the book publishers, describing your project and asking their permission to use the letters they published. It isn't necessary to contact the individual authors. To be on the safe side, you might also write to the publisher of the book written by the famous character himself, requesting permission to make use of that material. As for the descendants, there is the delicate question of the "right of privacy." Since each state has its own laws about this right, I think you might do well to consult a lawyer who could advise you how much latitude you have under law. Incidentally, a fact worth remembering is that Playwright-Producer Dore Schary paid $18,615 to Franklin D. Roosevelt, Jr. to compensate for "loss of privacy" caused by *Sunrise at Campobello*.

How Many Readers?

Q. I wonder if you could give me some idea of the way a book publisher handles an unsolicited manuscript. If the first person to read the book does not like it, does the manuscript go any further or is it rejected then and there? If he thinks it has possibilities, does it then go to a second and third reader, etc.? Also, does a standard rejection slip without any comment usually indicate that the manuscript did not arouse any interest at all with that particular publishing house?

A. The First Reader is as anxious to find a best-seller as you are to write one. Through her experience and training she is able to spot those manuscripts that show promise and those that do not. If she feels the book has no market potential at all, she will reject it then and there. If it has possibilities, it may be passed on to another reader or to an editor. By a process of consultation and elimination the marketable manuscripts are decided upon. A standard rejection slip can be taken to mean that on the whole, the publisher does not feel he could make money with that particular book, even though some member of his staff may have found some degree of merit in the work.

Novel, Magazine Length

Q. When writing a novel, magazine length (25,000 words), how does one go about beginning the first page? I don't mean the actual writing. I have it written. I want to know what goes on the first page. Is it the title, the second page a list of the characters, and the third, the first page of the first chapter?

A. The title page should have your name and address in the upper left-hand corner. In the upper right hand corner, state the approximate number of words, and the rights being offered for sale. Centered several spaces below that should be the title and your byline. Then about four spaces below that, center "Chapter One." Skip about three lines, and then begin your story. There is no need to list the characters.

Fiction Techniques

Q. For the past ten years I have been very active in religious work in a rural county. I desire to write up these experiences in book form. Each chapter will represent somewhat of a short story with a unifying overall story thread and quite a bit of local color. What effects can I use to heighten story interest?

A. Use plenty of dialogue, include vivid human-interest details, build a mood (through weather, landscape, etc.), try to create suspense by suggesting your own emotional reactions to a situation, and wherever appropriate, make a humorous observation about life in general as a result of some specific experience. Above all, keep your style lively and colorful so that readers will enjoy listening to your narrator. If you feel inhibited by the fact that your characters are actual living persons, you might have a freer hand if you fictionalize the events and make enough changes in the characters so that they become *your* literary creations, even though originally based on real people.

Time in the Novel

Q. I have had a novel in mind for almost ten years. My insurmountable problem is one of skillfully covering too many years without taking the reader's mind like a kangaroo on a long journey. Can you advise whether to 1) cut down on the number of years covered in the novel; 2) cut down on the detail during those years; 3) cut down on both of the above; 4) lengthen the novel to include both, then return later with a more skillful knife.

A. First you'll have to decide exactly how many years the story needs. If the same basic story can be told in either five or fifteen years, by all means choose the shorter period. Remember that for dramatic purposes, you can telescope events that might, in real life, be spread over several years. Regardless of how much time the story spans, you must be discriminating in your choice of detail. Don't include anything that does not keep the action moving forward toward the climax. Avoid all irrelevancies and descriptions for description's sake. Naturally the more important incidents will be developed in full scenes. But information of minor significance can sometimes be handled by brief transitional summaries that link the highlights together. There is also the flashback that can help a story make a time leap; but this technique should be used sparingly because too much hopping back and forth between the past and the present can create havoc with readers' time sense.

Fiction Techniques

Q. For the past ten years I have been very active in religious work in a rural county. I desire to write up these experiences in a book form. Each chapter will represent somewhat of a short story with a unifying overall story thread and quite a bit of local color. What effects can I use to heighten story interest?

A. Use plenty of dialogue, include vivid human-interest details, build a mood (through weather, landscape, etc.), try to create suspense by suggesting your own emotional reactions to a situation, and wherever appropriate, make a humorous observation about life in general as a result of some specific experience. Above all, keep your style lively and colorful so that readers will enjoy listening to your narrator. If you feel inhibited by the fact that your characters are actual living persons, you might have a freer hand if you fictionalize the events and make enough changes in the characters so that they become *your* literary creations, even though originally based real people.

Novel Outline

Q. In preparing an outline of a novel, just how much material should be in the outline? Would only a sentence or two, stating only the main event of the chapters be enough? Something like this: Chapter No. 5—Helen learns that John is secretly married to her sister, Marie?

A. The outline should be a little more detailed, suggesting scene changes and the specific action that leads to new developments (such as *how* does Helen discover this secret marriage). Remember, the outline has to be provocative enough to arouse the publisher's interest.

Chapter 18

Should You Use a Pen Name?

Anonymous Author?

Q. Can a writer use a pen name only, become successful or even famous, and still remain anonymous? This person dislikes publicity, and is very shy with the public or outside her family and friends' circle. What in your opinion would be the advantages and disadvantages of anonymity in such a case?

A. With the publisher's help, a writer could achieve both success and anonymity. The chief advantage of this would have to be the fulfillment of the author's own desire to remain unidentified. The disadvantages would include lack of public acclaim and the thrill of seeing one's own name on the book, the need to reject all interviews and photographs, and worst of all, the burden of having to keep a secret.

Pen Name Location

Q. If a writer uses a pseudonym, does he place it or his real name in the top left-hand corner of each page of his manuscript?

A. There is less chance of confusion when the real name is used in the upper left-hand corner of each page to identify the creator of the ms. Put your pen name on the title page as a by-line, e.g., "The Eye of the Beholder" by John Doe.

Check Cashing

Q. Sometimes an author writes under a pen name, because he doesn't want his real name known. How does one cash a check made out to his pen name—especially if he's well-known in a small town?

A. When the manuscript is submitted under a pen name, the author also usually includes his real name and address on the title page, so that the check will be made out to him and he can cash it without letting anyone know what the check is for. If, on the other hand, you mean the check is made out to the pen name, then the author can simply endorse it with the pen name and then endorse it over to his own real name and cash it that way.

Danger!

Q. Because I hope to begin my political writing where George Orwell (Eric Blair) concluded his career, I would like to adopt the pen name, George Orwell II. Will I need permission from his heirs?

A. Yes, you would need permission, but I doubt that Mr. Orwell's heirs would allow you to cash in on his reputation. Try to make it on your own!

Pen Name

Q. I am a patrolman on the Memphis Police Department, and since my stories often deal with policemen, I must for obvious reasons use a pen name. When submitting short fiction, is it desirable to include a short letter requesting the use of your pen name? Or would the cover sheet be used for this purpose? If I ever do sell anything, I would like to be able to cash my check.

A. In the upper left hand corner of your manuscript's first page, type your name and address, and your pen name in parentheses. Use this pen name as the by-line under the title, too. Then no letter is necessary.

Several Names?

Q. I love western adventure—have all of my life. I have the rough outline of three western stories, but it doesn't follow then that a fat woman of forty would have much appeal to western story fans. In other words they look for a book by a man—I do myself. Also I feel that I need different names for the different types of material I like to write, so it will not confuse the reader, or publisher, if I am lucky enough to get one. So I wish to adopt a pen name for my western stories, and perhaps a shortened form of my own name for science fiction, and gothic mysteries.

A. The only thing necessary for you to do in adopting several pseudonyns for the different types of writing you want to do, is to send a list of the names in which you might be receiving either mail or checks to both your bank and to your local postmaster, so that material will be safely delivered to you. The procedure on your manuscripts is this: type your legal name and address in the upper lefthand corner of the first page of the manuscript; underneath the title of your story, type the word, "by", and then list whichever pen name you prefer to use for that particular story.

Already In Use?

Q. I would like to use a pen name but my problem is this—How can I be sure the name I select isn't one that is already being used by someone else?

A. Except in the cases where extremely well known names, such as "Ann Landers" might be registered as a trade mark, most writers simply go to the Library of Congress Catalog card index in their public library, and look up the last name they want to use, and see if anybody else has already copyrighted books in that name. Your librarian could assist you in locating the directories of Library of Congress Catalog authors.

Value?

Q. Could you tell me, what is the real value of the pen name? Is it customarily used among professional writers today?

A. A pen name is used to protect the identity of the writer employing it. Of course, there are any number of reasons why a writer wouldn't want his real name associated with the material he writes. There might be a college professor of mathematics who secretly authors who-dun-its and doesn't want the word to get around to his students and colleagues. Or the writer's family might object to his career; and, to disassociate himself from them, he changes his name. Or the writer might simply dislike his real name—it may be hard to pronounce or look unwieldy in print—so he adopts a more suitable one. However, for most writers, there is sufficient satisfaction in seeing one's own real name in a byline.

Adopt a Real Name?

Q. I should like to use as a pen name a lovely name which happens to belong to a little girl in England, an occasional pen-pal of my daughter. Must I ask permission? What if I were to pick a name out of a telephone directory?

A. Yes, it would be best to ask permission of the little girl in England if you plan to use her name as a pen name in America. It's not a good idea to pick a name out of a telephone directory but rather to make up one that might be a combination of two different names.

Chapter 19

Submitting Photos With Manuscripts

Picture Sources

Q. In writing articles, I often need pictures for illustrations, and do not know where to get them. (I am not a photographer.) Of course, I should like them at a reasonable price or better still free. Also what sizes should I ask for?

A. For a list of free, or almost-free picture sources, see the article in the *1968 Writer's Yearbook*. These photographs can be used to supplement pictures shot specifically for your article by either 1) a professional photographer you engage for the purpose or 2) get to work with you on speculation.

Which Camera?

Q. What is a good camera to take along to photograph an interviewee? Is an expensive one necessary?

A. What do you consider an expensive camera? The twin lens reflex cameras that are manufactured by the Japanese (the Yashica is one) sell for about $50. This is an excellent camera for the beginner writer-photographer to use since it has a ground glass viewing screen which permits him to see exactly what he is taking a picture of.

Terminology

Q. One question that I can't seem to find a satisfactory answer to in my area is this: In the photo requirements, editors of magazines specify, they seem to use the terms "transparencies" and "slides" indiscriminately. That is particularly true in regard to the 35 mm color pictures.

A. Yes, editors use the terms transparencies and slides interchangeably.

How to Submit Transparencies

Q. Should Ektachrome (or other) transparencies be mounted, i.e., in the form of slides, when submitted to markets? And should they be enclosed in any special holder, or is a standard #10 envelope acceptable?

A. No, there aren't any *standard* procedures as I know for submitting Ektachrome transparencies to prospective magazines. Many photographers, however, do buy the 8 × 10 plastic holders in which Ektachrome transparencies can be slipped since this allows viewing of a quantity at the same time and yet still protects the transparencies.

Copyright

Q. A magazine is using a photo of mine (along with article) which I would like to copyright. Never before have I used a photo which I thought I wanted to protect, so am not sure how to go at this.

A. If you wanted to copyright a photograph of yours you would have to advise the editor in advance so he could publish the copyright symbol along side the photograph along with your name as the copyright owner. You would also have to write for the specific copyright forms from the Register of Copyright, Library of Congress, Washington, D.C., fill them out and return with the $6 copyright fee, and two copies of the published photograph.

Model Releases

Q. What information can you give me about necessary "releases" on subjects appearing in photos? All of my writing has been articles on business subjects in either selling or direct mail and I want to branch out into some outdoor articles but will undoubtedly have fish-

ing companions and guides in my photos so will need releases, etc.

A. A sample model's release appears in the *1969 Writer's Market* and a detailed discussion of when you need them and how to use them appeared in the Photojournalism column of the January, 1965, *Writer's Digest*.

Photo Pay

Q. Are photos—not carrying your credit—let us say, government photos, which you send with your article, purchasable by the editor? If photos are considered part of the purchase price, does the editor have to pay to use them? If so, who receives payment . . . the agency where you obtained photos, the photographer who took the pictures, or the writer who submitted them?

A. If you obtain some photographs free from the government and submit them to an editor, whether the editor wants to pay for them or not varies from magazine to magazine. If the magazine does decide to pay for them, they would include payment in the purchase price to the writer.

Picture Problems

Q. I might have the chance to interview some celebrities this summer. I cannot take the pictures, but there is a good professional photographer in this city who can. He is a complete stranger to me. Should I contact him before I query an editor or should I get the writing assignment first? If the editor does not purchase the story and pictures separately, what percentage does the photographer usually get?

A. Before you query the editor, explain your project to the photographer and see if he would be willing and available to furnish his services this summer. Reach an agreement with him regarding payment. (Being a professional, he will let you know his usual fees.) Then in your query to the editor, you can have the added advantage of informing him that you will be able to furnish professionally-taken photos of the interviewees.

Photo Details

Q. Could you explain the difference between $2\frac{1}{4} \times 2\frac{1}{4}$ and 4×5 transparencies?

A. Both refer to the size film used in the camera. Reflex cameras like the Rolleiflex, Yashica, etc., produce negatives, or transparencies that measure $2\frac{1}{4}$ inches by $2\frac{1}{4}$ inches. The Speed Graphic and Linhof, on the other hand, can produce negatives that are 4 inches by 5 inches. The $2\frac{1}{4}$ films are on rolls (size 120, 620, etc.) while the 4×5 is cut sheet film.

Photo Alterations?

Q. In a case where one of the branches of the military's promotional and public-relations department sends a news release with illustrating photo to the news media, is it OK for newspapers

to use one section of that photo (masking part of the persons) to illustrate a different news item?

A. It would be advisable for the newspaper to check with the military PR department on the use of that photo for a purpose other than was originally intended.

Photojournalist in Advertising

Q. How does a photographer go about breaking into the advertising business? Do the big companies that have page ads in the larger magazines give assignments or do they maintain a staff?

A. The big companies usually are clitheir accounts. Photographers frequently work on assignment directly from the advertising agencies. A photographer who wants to break into advertising would be wise to cultivate a contact at such an agency by showing samples of his professional work comparable to what the agency is already using.

Photo Return

Q. Can I expect to have unused photographs returned to me that are not used with an article? How can I indicate that I would like to have the unused ones returned? When they are not used, these photographs belong to whom?

A. The unused photographs belong to you and you are justified in requesting their return.

Chapter 20

How To Avoid Plagiarism

Quote How Much?

Q. In several articles I have written I quoted very briefly from hard cover editions the writings of several doctors, mostly psychiatrists. In most cases I referred to the doctor by name, and his book, and the publisher. Would you please be so kind as to fill me in on how much I can quote the works of others without writing for special permission?

A. There are no hard and fast rules on how much can be quoted from books without leaving one open to suits for copyright infringements. Some publishers say that, for example, if a whole poem is quoted, as few as fifty words may be a copyright infringement, while other publishers—especially in the scholarly field—say use a thousand words as long as you give proper credit to the author and publisher. One of the main thumbnail guides writers use in deciding how much they can use is to apply this question to their material, "Is what I am using impairing the sale value of the original?" From your letter, it sounds as though you are certainly well within your rights in the "fair use" of copyrighted material.

Free To Use?

Q. Some time ago my husband and I bought in an antique shop, a notebook of original poetry by Francis McAdams who died in 1942. Are we required to look up his descendants before publishing any of them or not? His most prolific year of poetry was 1931 and much of it has historical value. Could you give information on how to go about finding descendants if we need to?

A. Was the book that you have copyrighted? If so, it would have carried the copyright line on the fly leaf of the book. If it does appear, the copyright is in force for 28 years from the date of copyright. It also could have been renewed for copyright for another 28 year period, (and extended if expired since 1962). You are not at liberty to use any material from a book that has been copyrighted if the copyright is still in effect. If you are not sure and want to clarify whether or not the copyright is still in effect, you could write to the Register of Copyrights, Library of Congress, Washington, D.C. and try to find out whether or not a copyright is currently in effect on the book.

Similarity Breeds Suits

Q. I have been writing a vocabulary column which I would like to sell to some small newspapers. Without realizing it, my column is much like the monthly "Word Power" which is printed in the *Readers Digest* and is written by Wilfred Funk. In fact, although I am not using the words in his two books, *30 Days To A More Powerful Vocabulary* and *Six Weeks To Words Of Power,* my daily vocabulary tests in my written columns *resemble* the vocabulary tests used in these two books. Is there a copyright on Funk's "Word Power" column? If I went ahead and sold my newspaper column, would I have to get permission from Wilfred Funk Inc.? I stress this point: I am not using his *words,* but my test methods *resemble* his test methods.

A. If Funk's "Word Power" column is copyrighted, it probably carries the copyright notice somewhere near the title in the magazine. How closely your vocabulary tests resemble his, of course would be the crux of the matter as to whether or not you could be accused of copyright infringement. Best to consult an attorney for advice on this point.

Rewriting Songs

Q. I have written a song, taken from, and based upon an original poem. Some of the wording is different, while some of it is exactly the words of the original author. I would like to know if this is legal, and if not, how do I get the permission of the original author? Could I use the music from another original song, or do I also need the consent of the author of that music? I also have written "answers" to several hit songs. The words are different, but they fit the original music.

A. Neither the music from one song nor a number of words from another, can be used by you if the copyright is still in effect on either song. There is a directory available either in your local library—or at a nearby large library, which your local librarian could secure by an inter-library loan—called the *Variety Music Cavalcade.* This book lists songs by title and tells when the copyright was originally issued. It also gives the name of the publishing company to whom you should write to inquire about permission to use parts of the song.

Newspaper Features

Q. I have in mind an article about Christmas in a penitentiary for the December number of some magazine. I am an avid reader of the nearby Penitentiary News and have been for over 5 years. No, I am not a convict or an ex-convict. I've never been inside the pen, and the Warden denied my request to visit there to get material. My idea is to quote the prison *News* which is full of convicts' laments and their sad feelings of being behind prison bars on Christmas Day. I wrote the associate warden for permission to quote the *News,* and though he acknowledged it was in the public domain, I would have to get permission to quote each featured item. Here's his exact words: "Newspaper copy is in the area of public domain so that pick-ups of *news* from it may be made. Republication of *featured* items of the *News* however, would have to follow the usual routine of obtaining specific releases for each such item." If I had to go to all that trouble (specific releases for each item) the venture would not be worth it. If I ignored this warning would I stand to be sued or something? I don't want to get in the pen myself. That's for sure!

A. I'm afraid you have no choice but to write for specific releases for the feature articles by the inmates of the penitentiary or risk the possibility of suit. For further information on the copyright laws you might want to write to the Copyright Office, Library of Congress, Washington, D.C. and ask for a free copy of their general information booklet.

Plagiarism?

Q. For years I've been more or less avoiding nonfiction articles because I don't know where "research" ends and plagiarism begins. Where do you draw the line?

A. If long passages are lifted verbatim, then the writer has to get permission from the copyright owner. But don't let research scare you off. Ideas can't be copyrighted, so after you've dug up the facts, simply relate them in your own words.

Plagiarism?

Q. I read a story not too long ago in which the main character had many suppositions as to how his adventure would end. None was right. I would like to write a short story using one of these suppositions for my ending. However, of necessity, my story would have to be very close to the original. Is this plagiarism? Can I do it?

A. It is highly unlikely that the author would allow you to use *his* character in *his* story with a solution that *he* suggested. You'll find that originality is the best way of avoiding plagiarism.

Chapter 21

Writing For The Theater

Comparative Dialogue

Q. I am writing a play on an historical character. How would I incorporate exact quotations of this and other characters into my own dialogue. For example, in a Papal Brief I think I would have to use the exact words of the Pope and also the exact words of the reply, of personal letters, etc., that are in the public record. How would I do this and also use dialogue of my own creation?

A. Either steep yourself in the life and speech of that historical period to the point where there would not be any noticeable difference between the verbatim quotes and the dialogue you invent, as Arthur Miller seems to have done in *The Crucible*. Or impose your own style of speech on the period, paraphrasing the sources to make them sound compatible with your characters' dialogue, as in G. B. Shaw's *St. Joan*.

Play Agent?

Q. I have been writing one and two-act plays for little theatres. Is there a writer's guild? Is it necessary to send play manuscripts through an agent?

A. Yes, there *is* a Writer's Guild of America but it is for radio, television and film writers. There is the Dramatists Guild of the Authors League of America (234 W. 44th St., New York, N.Y.). There are many producers who do not require submission through an agent. For a list of these as well as producers who work only through agents, please see *Writer's Market* listing of "Play Producers."

Chapter 22

If You're a Poet

Poetry Definitions

Q. What is the difference between free verse and blank verse? Is rhyming in either necessary or optional?

A. Blank verse is unrhymed five foot iambic verse. Free verse does not follow any of the patterns of alternating accents and unaccents of metric verse. It sets up a music all its own which is neither a measured beat nor haphazard prose. As a general rule, lines that are not metric verse, accent verse or prose . . . are probably free verse. Free verse can be rhymed (as in some of Ogden Nash's work), but most frequently it isn't. Blank verse is not rhymed. For additional help with versification, consult *Wood's Unabridged Rhyming Dictionary.*

Manuscript Style

Q. I would like to know just what form my ms should be in when I am submitting a poem. Should the byline be just beneath the title or in the upper right hand corner?

A. Type your name and address in the upper left-hand corner. The title of your poem should be centered above the body of the poem. Your byline should be typed off to the right so that it ends about where your average line ends. Then you should center the poem on the page, with about equal distances above and below, and approximately the same margins to left and right. You should double-space short poems, but you can use single-spacing on long poems.

Resubmit?

Q. My great-grandfather was a poet and published a book of poems. He had only 300 books printed and gave them out to friends. The copyright was out years ago, over sixty years. There are some wonderful poems in this book and I would like to see them reprinted. Would it be legal to take out those and have them reprinted in magazines where every one could enjoy them. If this would be legal, then would I still use his name on them or my own?

A. You could try to bring these poems to the attention of current magazines, but under no condition would it be ethical to sign your name to them. They are the original work of your great-grandfather and should remain so.

Books of Poetry

Q. I have what I consider a worthwhile manuscript of poetry. Aren't there *any* publishers that would consider publishing it on a straight royalty basis?

A. Yes, there are publishers who have a regular royalty contract for poetry books, (see the *Writer's Market* list of "Book Publishers"). However, some of them hesitate to gamble on an unknown poet, and would prefer to publish poets with established reputations. To lay the groundwork for the possible future publication of your book, it would be helpful for you to get your poems published in magazines first.

Newspaper Poetry

Q. Does it make good sense to publish a poem in a newspaper—for a few dollars or maybe for free—and thereby lose all your copyright protection?

A. Most newspapers are copyrighted with an over-all copyright that covers the entire contents (other than straight hard news, which cannot be copyrighted, of course), so you don't lose copyright protection on poetry so published. If you contribute to a small weekly, of course, this may not be copyrighted, and it wouldn't be to your advantage to put your poetry in the public domain for a few dollars and lose the future use of the poem yourself.

Resell Poems

Q. A few years ago, I had a volume of poetry published at my own expense. Fortunately, there was a very good sale of this book. Now I would like to submit some poems published in the book to certain magazines, but have hesitated to do so as I'm not sure if this is permissible.

A. As long as the volume of poetry you had published at your own expense was copyrighted, then all rights to the poems still belong to you. It would be advisable to let the magazine editor know that your submission originally appeared in book form.

Modern Poetry

Q. I don't understand most modern poetry. Is there some book which has taken these kind of poems apart, analyzed them and discussed what the poet is saying?

A. Yes, *The Poet and the Poem* by Judson Jerome has chapters on this subject along with discussions of other matters of interest to poets attempting to become "professional" poets. What Mr. Jerome means by a "professional" poet as opposed to an "amateur" or "trade" poet is described in his column in the November, 1968 issue of *Writers' Digest*.

Book of Poetry

Q. Could you tell me what the procedure is for an author to sell a book of collected poems, if some of the verse has already been sold to magazines, and newspapers? Can he go ahead, and have the book published, or must he seek permission of the companies that published his verse?

A. Yes, the author who intends to collect his poetry, some of which has already been published, into a book, must seek permission from the companies that published the verses originally. There is usually no problem in getting permission, but it's necessary to write for it before producing the book.

Idea Borrowing

Q. One matter is bothering me. I have written and sold a poem based on an idea which I do not believe was original. Is such a borrowing considered unethical?

A. Set your mind at ease. Ideas cannot be copyrighted, so you have done nothing unethical.

Missing Authors

Q. I am writing a small book of poems, and I wish to include a few poems given to me by a friend. She told me the lady who wrote the poems never published them. Both my friend and the writer are dead. I tried to contact the writer's sister but the postmaster did not know her. Probably she has passed on. Should I use these poems in my book?

A. It is not advisable that you use the poems given to you by a friend, since their publication with the author's by-line might turn up some heirs who would frown on the use of this work. You seem to have made an effort to locate the author's sister, but I just wouldn't take a chance on a legal problem here for these few poems.

Chapter 23

Rules For Mailing

Postage Rule

Q. In the *Writer's Digest* you refer to sending manuscripts Special Fourth Class Rate—Manuscript (now 12¢ for the first pound and 6¢ for each additional pound or fraction). I think that in another column you gave the section of the postal code which applies to this rate. Would you be kind enough to give me that information?

A. The information you are looking for is in the "Postal Manual" under Postal Rule 135.13 and Section 135.214f. If a writer is challenged about using this rate by his local postmaster, he should notify the Post Office Department, Washington, D.C. 20540 and action will be taken to inform said local postmaster of the present rules and rates concerning educational materials.

Special 4th Class Mail Rate

Q. I have been mailing book manuscripts at this "Special Fourth Class Rate," and understand that article manuscripts qualify, but may short story manuscripts be mailed at this rate? Novelettes? Full-length novels? Book queries with outline and sample chapters?

A. The "Special Fourth Class Rate" may be used for any fiction or non-fiction manuscripts regardless of length, and also for sample chapters and outlines. If you enclose a letter, be sure you add 6¢ to the special rate of 12¢ for the first pound and 6¢ additional pounds, and mark the envelope "First Class Letter Enclosed."

Ed. Note:

Writers should also keep in mind that *unless* Special Fourth Class Rate mail is marked "Return Requested," the Post Office may destroy your manuscript if it happens to be mailed to an addressee who cannot be located.

New Name?

Q. I have submitted many articles and pictures over the years but at infrequent intervals I get the impression that some of the postal officials do not understand the accepted regulations concerning the mailing of manuscripts and photos. Just today I had a story and photos returned from an editor and the mailman required an additional 17 cents for it, although I had placed the required postage on the return envelope which was addressed to me. I had affixed a label and had rubber stamped the return envelope "Educational Material." I know that this carries another designation of late, but I had forgotten how it should be indicated.

A. The original designation of "Educational Materials" has now been changed to "Special Fourth Class Rate—Manuscript."

Chapter 24

In The Public Domain

Book of Poems

Q. You have given me the idea that my verses, which appear in a weekly uncopyrighted newspaper, are now in public domain. In order to incorporate them in a book of poems later, would I have to make changes in each one?

A. Yes, if you want to copyright your book, you'll have to produce a new version of the work because you cannot secure a copyright for something that is already in the public domain.

Erroneous Phrase

Q. Some periodicals indicate "Buys all rights. Publication not copyrighted." If a periodical is not copyrighted, it seems to me that the only rights it can claim are the rights to first publication. Am I right?

A. The publisher of an uncopyrighted publication may say "all rights" on his check; but it is true that the lack of copyright will permit anyone to make whatever further use of the material he wishes.

Government Hearings

Q. In writing an article which requires voluminous research, I am digging in every direction I can think of, in research of my own. However, I also have a book written by a reporter, I believe, and published by Simon and Schuster, which has been obviously thoroughly researched in ways which probably only a Press Card would allow and in which an unknown (myself) could not; it would be like beating my head against a brick wall, although I am trying to do the same. So I am wondering whether authorities which this reporter quotes—doctors, scientists, testifying before the Delaney Committee, would come under the heading of public domain—perhaps I could just as well have heard these same quotes myself; I don't know. In quoting these men, need I give credit to this book? To the editor? In the article? This article is for teen-agers. Is my knowledge of the facts now sufficient for making statements and/or paraphrasing or quoting scientists?

A. If the Delaney Committee you mention was an open hearing in Congress, then the material would be in the public domain and free for *you* to use, as well as the author whose book was published by Simon and Schuster. The Congressional Record for the date of the Delaney Committee Meetings would give you a printed version of their statements which you could use in your research easily. If, on the other hand, this Simon and Schuster author developed some of the quotes in his book from personal interviews with the experts, you would not be free to use this material. If you paraphrased and only used limited material, you would probably be safe under the "Fair Use" section of the copyright law by simply giving credit to the book and the author in your article. Extensive quotes however, would require that you obtain permission.

What's "Publication"?

Q. Each year our writers' club holds contests in several divisions: Short Story, Article, and various types of poetry. First, second, and third place winners, as well as honorable mentions, are announced in the published and unpublished divisions. As the procedure now stands, no method exists for exposing the winners' entries to the view of the league membership. We would like either a creative magazine with subscription limited to club members or to publish a year book with the same type of limited subscription. Objections reduce to a concern over copyright. Some members fear that such exposure of material would in effect make the writing public domain; or that a first rights sale to a paying magazine would be jeopardized.

A. The only way your contest entries could be made available to members is to copyright them and then print them either in a magazine or separately and send them out by direct mail. Whether or not this circulation to league members only would jeopardize the sale to a paying magazine, I just couldn't tell. Certainly unless you *do* copyright it, printing it even by mimeograph or multilith would put it in the public domain.

Quoting From Newspapers

Q. Can I quote personalities in the news who were quoted in daily newspapers and columns as having said such and such? Where can permission to quote be obtained? From the author? From the Newspaper—Book? or from the columnist? I collect inspirational sayings and want to publish this volume.

A. Since news cannot be copyrighted, if you are using quotations that are in *news* stories about personalities, you would not have to request permission. (I am assuming that the quotations were accurately recorded by reports and that they were not of a nature that the personality could subsequently sue for inaccuracy.) Most newspaper features and columns, however, are covered by copyright and you would not be able to lift quotations from these without requesting permission from the newspaper or the syndicate first.

Government Publications

Q. Is it permissible to quote directly from a document issued by the U. S. Government Printing Office? I have never been able to discover whether that material is copyrighted, or how credit should be given. Many of the leaflets would be very useful incorporated in articles or books, as well as in the preparation for writing on a subject. Do our taxes which pay for printing these items give us right to appropriate the words?

A. Yes, materials published by the U.S. Government are in the public domain. There are a few minor exceptions—some connected with the Post Office and some exceptions in which copyrighted material is inserted in the uncopyrighted public domain Government Bulletin. If you have any doubts about whether a specific leaflet you want to use is copyrighted or not, it is best to write the issuing government agency for clarification.

A. Unfortunately, once the material appears without copyright notice, it falls into the public domain and anyone may make whatever use of it he wishes. This would include reprinting it without notifying the author in any way.

Poem in an Uncopyrighted Magazine

Q. Does having a poem published in an uncopyrighted magazine entitle it to be reprinted without author's knowledge or consent?

Chapter 25

Publishing Procedures

Mysteries—How Long?

Q. A close friend insists an editor will not accept a mystery novel (not a who-done-it) if it exceeds fifty thousand words. My novel will exceed this amount by ten or twenty thousand words. Will an editor insist I cut my words to reach this requirement?

A. Editorial requirements are usually more flexible than your friend believes. Some publishers of mysteries will take seventy thousand words or more; for specific information, see "Book Publishers" in *Writer's Market*.

Always Keep a Carbon!

Q. When a magazine says "assumes no responsiblity for unsolicited material," does that mean the editors may not return a manuscript even if a stamped, self-addressed return envelope is provided?

A. The magazine will certainly try to send the manuscript back in its return envelope; but in case the manuscript or the envelope gets misplaced, the magazine waives any responsibility for getting it returned safely.

Reprint Buyers

Q. In the case of such magazines as *Reader's Digest*, do the editors of such magazines select the articles from perusal of various magazines or is it necessary for the author to submit a printed article which he feels might be suitable for reprint?

A. Though the editors usually select the articles for reprinting, an author may submit tearsheets to bring his material to their attention.

Vocabulary Lists

Q. I am interested in writing children's stories for the younger set. I am aware a word list must be in effect for Beginners Books. Where do I acquire such a list?

A. A two-part article on writing and selling the picture book for children appeared in our November and December 1967 issues of *Writer's Digest* articles, and Vocabulary is discussed on pages 50-51 of the December issue. While many publishers of *trade* books for children do not use formal vocabulary lists, publishers of *textbook readers* for the primary grades often have very formal restrictions on vocabulary based on studies made in elementary schools. Writers should familiarize themselves with readability formulas such as those developed by Dr. George D. Space and Dale-Chall. Consult the Education Dept. of your local public library and the publishers themselves for their own individual vocabulary requirements.

Single Copies

Q. I would like to obtain sample copies of a number of magazines not sold locally. To whom do I address such a request, and is payment expected?

A. Send your request to the editor, and offer to pay for the sample copy if necessary. Some magazines charge; others don't. Be sure to enclose a self-addressed stamped envelope in case they do need further correspondence with you.

Chain Publishers

Q. Various publishers issue several magazines from one address. There are cases where a publisher will issue several magazines, all of the same type, editorial style and content. They have different titles, though. In such cases, when a writer is submitting material for use in these magazines, is it considered by the editor concerned for *all* the magazines published by that company, even though it is addressed to one particular magazine, or is it in order to resubmit it for consideration for another magazine, even though it is published by the

same company? I ask this because I do not want to make the mistake of submitting material to more than one magazine published by the same company, if it is not proper to do so after having received a rejection from one of them. I am referring in particular to certain types of men's magazines such as *Men, Man's World, Male,* etc.

A. You are right. Certain editors head more than one magazine for their publisher, but from the same address. Also, an editor will pass along to another editor at the same company any story he can't use but thinks the other editor might.

Juveniles Seasonal?

Q. Is there one special time of year that material is read and accepted by publishers of children's books? If not, how far ahead should seasonal material be sent to them?

A. Most publishers read manuscripts the year round. Seasonal material should be submitted at least a year ahead of time.

Back to the Author?

Q. After a publisher accepts a manuscript, does he proofread it and send it back to the writer for corrections and retyping?

A. If you are talking about simple grammatical corrections, the publisher takes care of this and does not return the manuscript to the author for retyping. However, where substantial revisions of ideas or style are suggested, the manuscript may be returned to the author for additional work.

Special Meaning?

Q. Recently I sent a manuscript of a children's story to a publisher which was rejected. Instead of the usual rejection slip in the return envelope with the manuscript I received a separate letter saying they were sending my manuscript under separate cover. When I received it it was insured. I did not send it insured. Does this have any special meaning that my manuscript has any merit that would interest another publisher?

A. Some publishers just have the company policy of returning manuscripts insured. I think if the original publishing company to whom you sent it had any special comments to make on its merits, they would have said so in their rejection letter. Do not hesitate, however, to send it out to another publisher right away.

Buy Part?

Q. On recently submitting a 2,000-word article to a U.S. magazine, a few days later I received a letter of acceptance saying they were buying 500 words of the article at 5¢ a word and enclosing a check for $25. At first I thought of rejecting this offer, but as the article had been on the rounds for some time I decided against it. However, I am still not sure how I stand

on this matter. Is this a usual procedure? Or should a publisher pay for the whole article even if he only wants 500 words? And what about the remaining 1500 words; are they still my property to be offered for sale again by me?

A. Yes, a publisher who is not able to use a full article may offer to buy a part of it from the writer. If the writer accepts, then he agrees to the terms. The balance of the article can be sold to a *noncompetitive* market by the writer.

Reporting Time

Q. How long does a book publisher take to report on a ms?

A. The best you can expect is three weeks from the time you mail the ms. If you get a decision within a month after mailing, you are lucky. Seven weeks is average. Two months is not unusual. After that length of time, send a brief query, enclosing a stamped, self-addressed envelope.

Chapter 26

Sending a Query

Query?

Q. I am a newcomer to the wonderful world of writing and I am constantly confronted with the word: query. Is there a special or preferred form for a query? What is a query?

A. The query is a letter to an editor attempting to sell him on the idea of your article or book. It can be as short as a couple of paragraphs on one page or it could be two or three pages single spaced, depending on the complexity of the subject. Some samples of good and bad query letters to editors appear in the *1969 Writer's Market*.

No Answer on a Query

Q. If I send a query letter to an editor on an article idea and I don't get a reply, does that mean he's not interested?

A. No, the letter may have been lost. Be sure to enclose a self-addressed stamped envelope with your inquiry and, if you don't hear from the editor within a couple of weeks, don't hesitate to write a brief follow-up asking whether or not he's had time to consider your proposal.

Query First?

Q. Would like to ask about the "query first" which is always stressed. It seems so presumptuous for a beginning and unpublished writer to query first—how much attention would be paid them, anyway? I haven't yet had the nerve to try it.

A. A busy editor would much rather read a query to decide whether he's interested in a certain property than plow through a lengthy manuscript for the same purpose. From the writer's standpoint, think of the savings in postage and wear-and-tear on the manuscript. What *is* presumptuous is the writer who disregards an editor's stated request to "query first" and deluges him with completed manuscripts.

Chapter 27

What You May Quote

Permission to Quote

Q. I have read poetry written in response to a line from a magazine or newspaper in which the line is quoted above the poem. Is it necessary to obtain permission from the original source in order to quote the line?

A. If the material from which the line is quoted is under current copyright protection, permission must be secured. If the line is simply part of a straight news item, no permission is needed.

Use of Quotes

Q. Will you please explain the rules governing the use by writers of quotes and information gained from TV broadcasts? As a feature writer with an extensive clipping file, I have taken notes on some programs and speakers covering topics on which I am collecting information and leads into further research.

A. Generally speaking, if you accurately attribute your information to the proper source, you shouldn't run into any legal difficulty. In the case of direct quotations of *any length,* it might be best to write to the network or to the speaker, requesting permission to use the particular quotes.

Free to Use?

Q. In an original poem, I have said, "Good will upon earth, peace among men," which is based on the well-quoted phrase, "Peace on earth, good will to men," Is this legal?

A. The line you're paraphrasing is already in the public domain, so you don't have to worry on *that* score. For other phrases that might still have copyright protection, it would be advisable to reword the basic idea in your own way.

Phrase Borrowing

Q. Would you please discuss the ethics involved in an author's taking from one of his own published stories a sentence, a phrase, a simile, or anything for that matter—for use in another story.

A. The only prohibition would be the risk of having some alert readers tag you as belonging to that *New Yorker* category known as "Writers In Love With Their Own Words" Department!

Permission to Quote?

Q. To quote from publications of the U.S. Department of Labor, Commerce, Bureau of Standards, do I need permission from that Department?

A. Government publications (except a few allowed the Postmaster General) cannot be copyrighted, so you could quote freely—unless you are quoting already copyrighted material which happened to be part of a Government publication. When in doubt, always request permission.

Quoting Songs

Q. If you only mention the title, do you have to have permission from the song publisher? And what about old songs you quote from memory, like ballads or nursery rhymes, etc.? Must you find a publisher then and ask his permission? I plan to use quotes from some old lumberjack ballads and a few songs popular fifteen or ten years ago. I don't think a music store could help much on songs that old, could it?

A. You may mention a song title without having to get the song publisher's permission. As for old familiar folk ballads and nursery rhymes, if they are all older than 1909 they are in the public domain and can be used by anyone,

without permission. In the case of songs popular about fifteen years ago, however, their copyright will not likely have run out yet (length of copyright protection is 28 years and this may be renewed for another 28 years) so you probably need permission. Check for the publisher of popular songs by title in a directory available in most public libraries called the *Variety Music Cavalcade.*

Paraphrasing

Q. Must I write for permission from the copyright holder in order to paraphrase material, as with quoted material? When quoting from another book, may I omit surplus words such as "the," abbreviate or engage in other editing without using distracting dots to indicate such minor deletions?

A. No permission is needed for paraphrased passages, though sources of ideas should be acknowledged. The fact that a verbatim quote has been edited should, in all fairness, be indicated primarily to show readers that this is not exactly the way the author wrote it. The use of dots is the accepted practice, and not usually considered distracting.

Brief Quotes for Reviews Without Permission

Q. Many books have statements similar to the following: All rights reserved. No part of this book may be reproduced in any form without written permission from the publisher, except for brief passages included in a review appearing in a newspaper or magazine. May brief passages be quoted by reviewers in their reviews from books that do *not* bear similar statements?

A. Yes, even though books do not make this statement, reviewers may quote briefly from them under the "fair use" provision of the copyright law.

Permission to Quote

Q. I write articles for various dental trade journals and sometimes I write to people in the field for opinions regarding methods. I explain my intentions of writing an article concerning the subject of the information I'm seeking. Is it okay to use their correspondence in my article, or must I ask for their permission to do so?

A. Whenever the use of someone else's words and/or ideas is involved, it is best to request permission.

Permission to Quote

Q. I am writing a short story in which I am quoting excerpts from two major television commercials. I assume these advertisements are copyrighted. Is it necessary to obtain permission to use them?

A. When in doubt, the safest rule is always to ask permission to quote. Although slogans can't be copyrighted, a trade mark or patent can be registered for them.

Permission to Quote?

Q. I'm working on a 20th Century Journal-Notebook and would like to know how extensively I may quote from my reading (mostly contemporary fiction) without publisher's/writer's permission.

A. This type of quoting may become a legal problem since it concerns an interpretation of what the copyright owners feel is "fair use." To be on the safe side, you should request permission to quote the particular passages you intend to use in your Journal.

Chapter 28

How To Find Facts

Library Research

Q. In doing research in libraries for story material, copying long passages is a slow laborious job. Is there any known method that is faster?

A. Talk to your local librarian about the availability of copying machines (such as Xerox) or perhaps about photostating the material you need.

Historical References

Q. I am writing a short story based on a colorful but for the most part unheard of, or forgotten, figure of the 1820's. I studied a dozen or more library references to get the information I needed. How should I give credit without typing half a page to list my source of knowledge?

A. In order to give credit where it is due and provide your story with the proper authentication, you should include a bibliography of source material even though it might take up "half a page." Your editor can then decide how much to include.

Poetry Reference

Q. I have just written a novel and am about to submit it to a publisher. My title is taken from a stanza learned many years ago; but I am unable to locate the source or author.

A. You might try searching this out through either the Poetry Index or the Essay and General Literature subject index in your local public library. Also the *New York Times Book Review* features a column of "Queries and Answers," and you might be able to track down the source of the poem by addressing the Queries Editor, *New York Times Book Review,* New York, N. Y. 10036. Include a self-addressed, stamped envelope for reply.

Government Addresses

Q. Presently, I am researching a highly controversial article which requires positive statistical support from numerous government agencies. It is important that the agencies give the information, 'from the horses mouth', for record purposes. Where exactly, may I get the correct mail address of the parent departments and subordinate bureaus of the government?

A. The U.S. Government Organization Manual is probably in your local library. This publication will give you the current addresses of the various departments and bureaus of the government.

Permission to Include

Q. In doing a "round-up" article should I have the consent of the individuals whom I include? If the information may be gathered by other than personal interview? What I have in mind are actors with some background trait in common, etc. Also, is it professional to interview by mail when your subject is out of your local vicinity?

A. Yes, it is best to have the consent of the individuals whom you would include in a 'round-up' article. Yes, many writers do interview by mail or phone when the subject is out of their local vicinity. If you haven't already read it, you might want to refer to the *1966 Writer's Yearbook* which is probably available in your local public library since it contains an article on how to handle the 'round-up' piece.

Reference Source

Q. I would appreciate any information that you may have concerning children's periodicals—their history, developments, uses, etc.

A. If you will check in your local library for a directory called the *Subject Guide to Books in Print,* there, under Children's Literature—History and Criticism, you will find a number of books listed that may be of help to you.

Sunrise? Sunset?

Q. I have lived in many different places in the U.S. and also briefly overseas. Sometimes I like to use these various places as settings, but I find it very difficult to remember the hours of sunset and sunrise. Is there a book that lists such facts?

A. The exact times would seem to be unimportant to any stories you might wish to write, but you can check in the *American Ephemeris and Nautical Almanac* which gives these times for every fifth day. You would, of course, have to first determine the latitude of your setting from a map.

Interviewing Non-Experts

Q. I am interested in learning how to interview people. Not just celebrities, but ordinary people too. I need their opinions and answers to questions for several articles I am working on. Do you just walk up to people and ask them? Do you have to have some sort of credentials? Do you need a release on the material they give you? Do you have to name them in an article, or are you not supposed to name them? Do you have to pay them?

A. Yes, a lot of freelance writers just walk up to people and ask them if they can interview them briefly on some research material they are seeking. No, writers do not usually pay the people they interview. No, it is not necessary to name them in the article unless they are authorities whom you are quoting and it would lend credence to your article to quote them specifically by name. If you do quote them specifically by name then, yes, you do need a release on the material they give you.

Science Fiction Writing

Q. Are there any books available pertaining to the writing of science fiction?

A. Yes, there is the *Science Fiction Handbook* (The Writing of Imaginative Fiction) by Lyon Sprague De Camp. A more recent discussion is Kingsley Amis' *New Maps of Hell* (Harcourt, 1960, $3.95). Then too, in many science fiction anthologies, there are introductions that offer insight into this specialized field.

Thank You Notes Necessary?

Q. I am doing research for an article by writing letters to many companies across the country. Many have written detailed answers to me and given me much information that I might not otherwise have gotten. Is it customary or polite to answer each one of these with a thank you? This could run into quite a bit of correspondence for me,

but I do feel that I owe these people some thanks for their cooperation. What do you say?

A. Thank you notes are not obligatory in this case, but they would certainly be welcomed and appreciated. You may, if you wish, send the helpful companies tearsheets of your article when it's printed, along with a thank you for the information they contributed.

Old Photos

Q. I have a lot of difficulty in locating pictures for many of my stories. I have found one source, Wide World Photos, but have written several football articles on some of the great teams of the past. Do you know how I could acquire pictures for my stories? Do you know of any other source for photos?

A. One of the best sources of historical photographs is the Bettmann Archive, Inc. whose address is: 136 East 57th Street, New York, N.Y. 10022. Several others are listed in the article on "Picture Sources" in the *1968 Writer's Yearbook*.

Books By Mail?

Q. There are some books I'd like to read, but they're not in our local public library. Is there anyplace I can borrow these books from so I don't have to buy a copy of each one?

A. Most public libraries participate in a plan called inter-library loan. That is, if you want a book that your library does not have, they will borrow it from another library for you charging you only the postage to get the book and return it. I suggest you inquire of your local librarian of this plan.

Organizing Problems

Q. I need help on researching and then organizing all my material before I actually sit down to write an article. I spend so much time shuffling papers around I never can get started writing.

A. How the professionals do it is described in *A Treasury of Tips for Writers* by the Society of Magazine Writers ($4.50) along with their ideas on other subjects such as interviewing, keeping records and, of course, writing.

Reference Source

Q. How can I find out any information on Language Arts in the second and third grades?

A. A public library near you probably has a reference book called *Subject Guide to Books in Print,* where you could find under the category "Language and Languages" some books that would be helpful.

Obtaining Permission

Q. Is the writer of a how-to book required to obtain permission to use names and addresses in the following respects: Names and addresses of sources of equipment and supplies necessary in executing the project being ex-

plained in the book ... and ... titles of books recommended for supplementary reading, together with the authors' and publishers' names.

A. It is not necessary to request permission for use of the titles in your Bibliography, but you might wish to check with the suppliers for permission to include their names and addresses in your reference list.

Playing Time

Q. In Stanley Richards' article (March, 1967 *Writer's Digest*) he covered many helpful areas for beginning playwrights. But there remains one aspect—time per page of dialogue—which goes unanswered.

A. The average playing time of a twenty to a thirty minute one-act play is twenty to thirty typewritten double-spaced pages. A one and one-half to two-hour full length play usually runs ninety to one-hundred and twenty double-spaced typewritten pages.

Chapter 29

Those Rejection Slips

Comments on Rejection Slips

Q. On recent rejection slips from greeting card companies were handwritten "terrific possibilities but more punch" and "ideas good but lack sales appeal." I am in the dark as to what comprises "punch" and "sales appeal." Should I take these handwritten remarks on form rejections to be encouraging or do editors often write in remarks?

A. These handwritten nutshell criticisms certainly should be regarded as encouraging. By referring to "punch" and "sales appeal," these editors probably meant that your work lacked the impact necessary to make the prospective card buyer immediately react favorably to the cards. It would seem, then, that your underlying ideas are good, but you need to present them in a more colorful, more entertaining or dramatic way that will catch the customer's attention and make him buy.

Rejected?

Q. I recently received my first story back. It did not have the usual printed rejection slip attached. Instead, I received a short personal note telling me they were overstocked and I should not submit material until late August. Was my story rejected completely or should I feel it *was* adequate for their magazine?

A. It is possible that your story was not even read, but that it was automatically returned because the market is so overstocked at present. You should resubmit the story in late August, as they suggested, since the note seems noncommittal about rejecting or accepting it.

119

Chapter 30

Reprints Double Your Sales

Re-submitting Articles

Q. Over the years, I have contributed a great deal of material to our local natural history group's mimeographed magazine, gratis. Would it now be permissible to sell some of these articles? If so, is it necessary to tell the prospective buyer that it has been used, and the details?

A. Since your mimeographed magazine presumably is not copyrighted, all the material it contains is in the public domain, which leaves you free to make whatever use of it you wish. However it would be ethical to advise prospective buyers where and when the articles first appeared. If you significantly rewrite these articles, then mention of former publication would not be necessary.

Selling Your Story Twice

Q. I have sold a Christmas story. Now could I legally try to sell this same story to other juveniles accepting simultaneous submissions, as mentioned in Dave Hill's article in your *1965 Writer's Yearbook?* Or does this apply only to articles? If I may do this, where

would be the proper place to indicate "simultaneous submissions" or "sold to so-and-so"?

A. Multiple submissions may be made for fiction as well as nonfiction in the field of religious markets. Place a note about such submissions and/or previous sale in the upper right hand corner of the first page of your manuscript.

Clippings

Q. How would I obtain permission to publish items and articles that I have clipped from newspapers over a period of time? Would permission from the newspapers be enough—or would I have to go to the source, the wire services?

A. It depends on what you're clipping and who owns the copyright. Straight news items cannot be copyrighted, but certain syndicated columns and wire service exclusive interviews are. Write to the newspaper first, requesting permission to publish their items and they'll advise whether further correspondence is necessary. The addresses of the two major wire services are: The Associated Press, General Office, 50 Rockefeller Plaza, New York, N.Y. 10020; and United Press International, General Offices, News Building, 220 E. 42 St., New York, N.Y. 10017. The names and addresses of other wire services may be found in the *Editor and Publisher Year Book.*

Reselling Your Story

Q. Would you please tell me how I would sell a story to a magazine so that I may sell to a number of magazines?

A. The first time you sell a story, specify First Serial Rights Only, then all secondary rights will belong to you and you can try to resell this story to another magazine that will use previously published material. You should naturally inform such subsequent magazines where and when the story originally appeared.

Serial Rights

Q. About ten years ago, I sold a story to *Modern Romances.* There was no mention of serial rights but the check I endorsed stated they were buying all serial rights. Can I now sell second serial rights to another publication?

A. Since the magazine bought all rights, the second serial rights are no longer yours to sell.

Prison Paper Reprint

Q. I am an inmate of a state prison. If I sell a story to a religious magazine, can I in turn "give" it to our prison paper to print? Our prison paper is not a copyrighted paper.

A. If the religious magazine is not copyrighted, then you may "give" the story to your paper. If the magazine is copyrighted and buys all rights, then I'm sure you'll be able to make some arrangement with them for the reprint of the story in your paper.

Adapt a Poem?

Q. I feel that a certain narrative poem written in the 1800's but found in a school textbook with a 1963 copyright, could be adapted into a fine play, especially for television. Must the playwright secure permission to make such an adaptation?

A. It would be best to check with the publisher on the copyright protection of this poem. Even though the poem was written in the last century, its present appearance might be its first publication, in which case the copyright would make permission necessary.

Resell Another Way?

Q. An original party plan, which I recently sold to a leading children's magazine, included a novel idea for a party invitation. Do the rights purchased by the magazine prohibit me from selling the invitation to a greeting card company?

A. If the children's magazine lists which rights it buys in the *Writer's Market,* or indicated which rights it buys on the check you received for the plan, that is your answer. If you're not aware exactly what rights the magazine did buy, then by all means drop them a note and clarify this point before you resubmit your idea to a greeting card company. Although ideas themselves cannot be copyrighted, the particular presentation of the idea—in this case, a party invitation—could be covered by copyright.

Resell Idea?

Q. I recently came across an old story of mine published in a senior high magazine. It seemed quite good and I think with a little updating and a slightly different twist at the end it would be suitable for *The American Girl* or similar magazine. Would there be any reason I could not do this?

A. Since you do intend to revise the published story, it would be all right to market it as a new work for current magazines.

Weekly Articles

Q. Recently I wrote several articles for a small, semimonthly, rural area newspaper. As I received no compensation, must I get a release from the publisher if I wish to submit a slightly revised version to nationally-known magazines?

A. Since there was no exchange of money, there was probably also no statement by the publisher that he wanted further rights to any of the material he obtained from you. Unless you had any kind of limiting agreement such as that described above, I'd certainly go ahead and try my luck in the national market-place.

Pre-Ann Landers?

Q. Just recently, while cleaning out a very old writing desk, I came across a section of an old newspaper, which is nearly 50 years old. While scanning the section, which turned out to be a question and answer deal, such as we have today like Ann Landers and Dear Abby, I found to my great amusement, some of the funniest questions and answers I have seen in a long time. Most of the questions dealt with dresses, hair styles and questions like "Am I of the right size?" Here some sizes were given, such as 42-27-37, plus the weight and height. I would like to submit these for sale, but know of no outlet for them. Would you please advise me on how these should be typed and also where I could send them.

A. If the Question and Answer Section of the old newspaper was copyrighted, as are Ann Landers and Dear Abby today, you would not be free to use this material. Since, if the copyright were renewed it would be valid for 56 years (or more, if it expired since 1962) you would have to take this into consideration. If the column was not copyrighted, you would be free to submit this material to filler markets which might be interested in the subject matter. *The Writer's Market* lists innumerable magazines and tells what kinds of filler material they buy. These filler items should be typed one to a page with your name and address in the upper left-hand corner, the date and source of the item beneath the item and the manuscript accompanied by a self-addressed stamped return envelope.

Re-use Without Permission?

Q. For several years, in addition to my free-lance writing, I have edited a monthly bulletin for a club of which I am a member. I have recently been thinking of gathering all of my bulletin material and publishing it in a small book. Each issue of the bulletin is published with the sentence, "Permission to reprint material from this bulletin is granted provided proper credit is given." May I legally gather and print my material without permission from the club? I intend to make it very clear that the material came from the bulletin.

A. I think it would be best to clarify with the club of which you are a member that you plan to reprint material which you originally edited in their monthly bulletin. I think it will save you headaches later if you clear this with everybody first. You will be pointing out, of course, that the bulletin will be credited, and that's their main concern, but it's best to tell them first.

Story into Book?

Q. If a children's story has been accepted and published in a magazine, is it possible to gain permission to offer it to a book publisher for publication as a picture book? If so, what procedure should be followed?

A. Yes, a published story can be turned into book form provided the author has retained the book rights. You will need to check with the magazine to ascertain which rights were purchased along with the story. If they bought *all* rights, then you'll have to try to make some special arrangement concerning the book rights. If, on the other hand, you own these rights, submit your story to the book publisher and be sure to inform him of its previous publication.

Revise and Sell Publicity Features?

Q. As a publicist I write and send feature stories to newspapers which frequently use the material verbatim. If I should select a better than average piece, delete the commercial overtones and send the story to a magazine, where do I stand legally and ethically?

A. I see no reason why you couldn't resell revised versions of feature articles to magazines you wrote originally as a publicist and placed in local newspapers. Although you remove the commercial overtones, the company's industry in general would probably benefit from the national coverage, so I don't see what objection they would have to that.

Poetry Resubmitted

Q. About twenty years ago, I had a book of poetry published. Can I now send these poems around to markets, and should the book be mentioned? I also write two columns for free. Should these be copyrighted?

A. If you own the serial rights to your book of poems, you are free to try to sell them to magazines that do use reprints; but you should mention the book in which they originally appeared.

If your columns appear in an uncopyrighted publication, then you should see to it that they are accompanied by a notice of copyright in your name, and you should write to Register of Copyrights, Library of Congress, Washington D.C. 20540 for Form BB—"Contribution to a Periodical Manufactured in the U.S."

American Re-Sale?

Q. I have sold some verses and articles to a British magazine and would like to try to sell them to American publications also. Can I still offer First North American Rights? Should I make mention of the fact that they have already been printed in Britain?

A. It would be fair to advise the American publications of the British sales record of your material. You would also need to check with the British magazine which bought your work to find out what rights, if any, they still retain to this material.

Story Rewrite

Q. Two years ago a short story of mine appeared in my high school's literary magazine which is published annually by the school and contains work submitted by students only. Recently I have added more to the story and changed some of the beginning, but the majority of what appeared in the magazine is still the same. I would like to know if this work is considered a published manuscript. I would like to try

to sell it, but most magazines want short stories not previously published.

A. Yes, your work has been "published"; but since the school magazine probably wasn't copyrighted, and since you have revised the story, thereby technically producing a new work, you are free to try marketing the *new* version as an unpublished manuscript. (**Ed. Note.** Writers are reminded that "publication" in an uncopyrighted magazine places "that" version of their work in the public domain.)

Multiple Sales?

Q. Recently a photographer asked me to write copy to go with his pictures. To date we have completed two Sunday pictorial articles. Now he wants to resubmit these sold articles to subsequent markets. Can we keep reselling them to different newspapers and magazines?

A. You will have to check on what rights were bought by the original Sunday pictorial. And, of course, resales should be to noncompeting magazines and newspapers.

Chapter 31

Rights and Copyrights

Rights Question

Q. What is the difference between First North American Rights and First Serial Rights Only when submitting to a major magazine?

A. Both phrases are usually taken to mean the same thing, namely the right to publish the material once for the first time. The word "Serial" refers to newspapers, magazines, etc., that are published on a continuing basis. First North American Serial Rights covers first publication rights in both the U.S. and Canada and American magazines which distribute in Canada usually want this extra protection.

Defunct Magazine

Q. I sold a short story to *Climax* magazine, which is now defunct. Who owns the story now? Can I submit it to a reprint magazine?

A. The publisher who bought the story would still own it for as long as his copyright is valid. Your right to submit it to a reprint magazine would depend on what rights you originally sold.

Rights to Fiction Characters?

Q. Does the character and the name of the character belong to the copyright owner, or the story itself?

A. It is customary for the character to belong to the copyright owner. There is a notable court case involving Dashiell Hammett's selling of motion picture rights in *The Maltese Falcon* to Warner Brothers. After this sale, Hammett then granted CBS the right to use Sam Spade, the leading character in *The Maltese Falcon*. Warner Brothers sued but *lost*. Since then, movie companies now make their contracts more specific about wanting the rights to certain characters as well as their stories and titles. You, as the author, might specify your wish to retain the rights to your characters.

Subsidiary Rights

Q. What rights do I sell on my book?

A. The logical thing to offer is "book rights only." but, if you are a beginner, you are in a tough bargaining position regarding movie, syndicate, paperback and book club rights. But try to hold on to as many of these rights as possible. In the *1967 Writer's Yearbook* article, "What the Beginner Should Look For In His First Book Contract," the editor recommended that the author's share of subsidiary rights should be *no less* than 75% on foreign editions, 50% on paperback and book club sales and 90% on TV and movie sales.

Revise vs. Original?

Q. About five years ago, I sold a children's story to a magazine which greatly altered and shortened it. It was published with a credit line which said, "adapted from a story by Joseph P. Ritz." There is no question the magazine owns the publication rights to the story which was published. But does it also own the rights to the original manuscript, to date unpublished?

A. The story the magazine paid for was your original one, which they were then entitled to change as they saw fit. Sorry, but this story no longer seems to belong to you unless, by agreement with the publisher, you retained certain rights in it. If you're not sure, write the original publisher.

Quoting Lyrics

Q. In my story it would help add realism to use the titles of a few popular songs, and some "snatches" of the lyrics (as being played by the orchestra or coming from the juke box). Would it be necessary to get permission or give credit for this use?

A. If you're going to quote directly from the lyrics, then you will definitely need the music publisher's permission. A list of publishers of popular songs appears in a directory (available in most public libraries) called *Variety Music Cavalcade*.

Trade Names

Q. In a short story I've just completed, I have used the trade names Zyglo and Magnaflux, which are the property of the Magnaflux Corporation. The reference is only used to give authenticity to the lead character who is a factory worker. There is nothing derogatory connected with it. Am I legally required to secure permission from the company to make such a reference?

A. There should be no objection to your fair use of these trade names, but it wouldn't hurt to drop a note to the companies involved, anyway.

They're Yours for the Taking

Q. Recently I wrote a short story as an assignment for a correspondence course I'm taking. When the assignment came back, a number of specific word changes were suggested. Can I legally use the wording suggested by the instructor in these instances?

A. Feel free to appropriate revisions of correspondence course instructors. They lay no claim to any word changes made as part of the teaching process.

Vox Populi

Q. Having read an article in a small magazine, which I did not approve of, I would like to answer with an article of my own in a newspaper. Would it be permissable to use the same title only for my new article or should I use a new title and mention the old one somewhere through the article?

A. By all means create your own new title, and if you wish, mention the other one in the body of your article.

Exposé Problems

Q. I am in the process of writing an exposé-type book. Since the materials which I plan to expose are copyrighted, obviously I cannot quote from them without the permission of the authors. I doubt that any author would consent to my using his material to prove a point against himself. How do I go about doing this legally?

A. Remember that copyright protects only the exact wording of a passage. One way of accomplishing your goal without

"All" Rights

Q. What does "Buys all rights" mean? Does it mean they buy first, second, another way of saying "Exclusive"? Or that they buy any rights offered?

A. "Buys all rights" means that they buy the rights to *all* the possible avenues of sale on that manuscript—such as book, movie, TV, etc.

Photocopy?

Q. Most books now carry the legend: "No part of this book may be reproduced or utilized in any form or by any means, electronic or mechanical, including photocopying, recording or by any information, storage and retrieval system, without permission in writing from the Publisher." Does this mean that a writer, with access to a dry photocopier, is not allowed to reproduce a page or portion thereof for his private research file without first getting the permission of the publisher?

A. If the reproduction of a text is just for your own private research file, then it would be all right to use the photocopier the same as it would be to copy the facts in longhand. However, if any of your manuscripts submitted for publication are going to use a verbatim quote from such material, you would need permission.

Ms Rights

Q. Will typing First North American Rights on a manuscript still assure the author of retaining all other rights? If an editor's acceptance check is stamped All Rights after you have specifically offered to sell him only First Rights, can you write, returning the check, and object without jeopardizing the sale?

A. In addition to specifying on the manuscript, the rights you are offering for sale, you may also include a note in which you clearly indicate the rights you wish to retain. If the acceptance check is stamped *All Rights* and you

127

object, you may return the check with a very tactful letter in which you outline the rights you prefer not to sell. Of course, there is always the chance this may jeopardize the sale (especially if purchasing all rights is the publisher's established policy), but if you are strongly opposed to yielding all rights, then this is a risk you'll have to take. Publishers can be reasonable, though, and you might be able to make a special arrangement concerning the assignment of rights. But this should be done prior to endorsing the acceptance check.

Cook Book Problems

Q. I am compiling a specialty cook book. Some recipes are original, others have been gathered from various publications. Is it necessary to list the source of each recipe, or may I just call it a collection of recipes? If I change the amount of an ingredient or add a new ingredient, may I call it an original recipe? On this type of manuscript, would editors rather have a query alone or a query accompanied by an outline?

A. If you are quoting the recipes verbatim from copyrighted publications you will need permission. A change in ingredients and new description of procedures would make it a new recipe. A query *and* outline would be preferable when submitting to a book publisher.

"Best" Rights?

Q. What are usually the best rights and/or most profitable rights offered by writers of short stories and books?

A. Most magazines list in publications like *Writer's Digest* and the *Writer's Market* the rights they buy on short stories. If they don't indicate a specific type of rights they buy, the best thing the writer can do is to list in the upper right hand corner of the first page of his manuscript "First North American Serial Rights Only". This gives the magazine the privilege of printing the story once with all other rights remaining with the author. As far as books are concerned this is a very complicated arrangement and individual with each book and author. You might want to read the *1967 Writer's Yearbook* which contains a feature article called "What the Beginner Should Look For In His First Book Contract".

Poem Rights

Q. I have been sending in a little article each week to a newspaper in which I use a poem (not composed by me) along with Bible scripture and a few words of my own. Am I allowed to use this poem?

A. If these poems come from books, for example, whose copyright is still in effect, you will definitely need permission to quote them.

Permission to Quote?

Q. In writing an article, is it legal to quote from the sources occasionally and give credit in a footnote or is it necessary to get the permission of each author or publisher the writer quotes from?

A. If the quotes are short enough they would come under the copyright principles of "fair use," and no permission is needed. The footnotes would be a good idea.

"Rights" Problems

Q. Is it necessary to write for permission from each publication who has published my poems, in order to compile a book of poetry from my published work? Some have indicated that they had bought first rights only—does this automatically give permission to sell or publish again? And if some are written under pen names, may they be republished under the same name or can they be published under my own name?

A. If you sold only "First Rights," then you own the book rights, but they are held in trust for you by the original publisher and he must be contacted. If there are some instances where you're not sure what rights were purchased, you'd better check with the publisher. Though written originally under pen names, the poems may now be presented under your own name. Your projected book should contain a List of Acknowledgments, indicating where these poems first appeared.

What Rights?

Q. While most "how to" books advocate specifying rights for sale on mss, one popular seller claims this is a mark of amateurs, and that editors who buy other than what is offered might reject for this alone rather than dicker over rights. What is the accepted practice?

A. It is customary and business-like to offer First Serial Rights unless the magazine's editorial listing in the *Writer's Market* flatly states that it only buys all rights. Then the writer has to decide whether he wants to sell under those terms.

Rights Infringement

Q. Since ideas can't be copyrighted, would it be necessary to obtain permission from the author of a short story before expanding the material to book length?

A. According to "A Copyright Guide" by Pilpel and Goldberg (R. R. Bowker Company), copying the exact wording of a copyrighted work is not the only method of infringement. Infringement would also cover the copying of the development, treatment, arrangement or sequences of ideas and facts included in the work. Therefore you are not at liberty to base a book on another author's short story without the consent of that author.

Rights Unknown

Q. Eleven years ago I sold a juvenile story to a now defunct children's magazine called *"Tom Thumb's Magazine for Little Folks."* In their acceptance letter they did not mention the rights they were buying and I cannot remember what I signed on the back of the check. Since I understand now that children's stories can also be sold as books, if the author retains book rights, how may I find out what rights I do have?

A. You should try to locate, through the Copyright Office, the last known address of the copyright owner and check with him on the ownership of book rights. But first it might be helpful for you to secure the free government circular No. 22, which deals with such Searches. Address: Copyright Office,

Foreign Copyright

Q. I am curious to know if a word-for-word translation of any foreign language book without the publisher's consent is considered plagiarism?

A. If the foreign language book is copyrighted, it may *not* be translated without the consent of the copyright owner.

Definition

Q. What is meant by "rights"? What rights are you supposed to sell?

A. A writer is entitled to decide who shall own the right to print his story for the first time or reprint it or make it into a movie, etc. Such rights are his protection against those who would come along and freely use his work for their own purposes and gain. The rights most commonly offered for sale are First North American Rights, which means the writer is selling the publication the right to be the first to print this particular work just once. All the other rights still belong to the writer. On the manuscript, in the upper right hand corner of the title page, indicate these rights you are offering for sale.

Title Rights?

Q. In July 1958 I sent a manuscript to the Macmillan Company. They rejected (as did others) after keeping it so long it was necessary to write them about it. Now I read they are publishing a book by that exact title. The title is extremely important to my book. Do *they* have all the right in this case?

A. A title cannot be copyrighted. But it *can* be protected under the rules that prohibit unfair competition which would prevent a publisher from bringing out a book with a title that's the same as a recent best-seller. Actually, there's nothing stopping you from keeping your title, especially if your story is completely different from the published one with that title.

Adapting Classics

Q. I am interested in adapting stories by Dickens, Hawthorne, and Washington Irving for TV. How can I determine whether or not this material is in the public domain?

A. Copyright protection runs for 28 years and may then be renewed just once for another 28 years. Any copyrighted material that is over 56 years old (except for material whose copyright expired since 1962 which has been renewed by Congress while it is considering a new Copyright Bill) would now be in the public domain.

Too Much!

Q. After reading a novel I enjoyed, by a famous author, I decided to write a continuation of that novel. Of course, I will have to use the author's characters, and to hold the same atmosphere, I will have to describe them as he did —same habits, speech, etc. Also, because of the characters recalling their past, I will have to use some of the author's situations and his characters' dialogue. Do you feel that I would be asking permission for too much?

A. I assume that the original work is still under copyright protection. If so, then indeed you do seem to be asking permission for too much, and I doubt if you will get it!

Permission Problem

Q. I wrote a sonnet inspired by a column by Bishop Sheen, and wonder now if I must get permission from him to submit it for publication. The first seven words (first line) of the sonnet are also the first seven words of the column, and the poem expresses some of his ideas (in my words).

A. While it's all right to use the Bishop's prose as inspiration for your sonnet, you should secure permission to quote those first seven words of his column.

Rewrite Tennyson?

Q. Recently, I rewrote a poem of Alfred Lord Tennyson's, using only a few of his original stanzas and took the viewpoint of the woman rather than the man he had written about. What I want to know is this: Can this sort of thing be published? If so, what type market would consider it?

A. Lord Tennyson's work is in the public domain, so you are free to write your own version of that poem. Since you do not indicate which poem it is, or whether your version is an amusing parody or a serious poem, it is difficult to suggest markets. But since appreciation of your poem would probably depend on the reader's familiarity with the original, I would recommend submission to some of the quality, literary, or quarterly magazines such as *American Weave*, etc.

Copyright Question

Q. I have an old book that has lost its cover and the first 144 pages. I have no way of knowing the author, publisher or date. It contains very specific accounts of Indian battles, giving dates and names of the Chiefs involved and the settlers. Could I offer these tales to a publisher? How would one find a publisher for this early Americana?

A. I suggest you write to the Copyright Office (Library of Congress, Washington, D.C.) requesting their free circular #22 entitled "Searches" which deals with the problem of determining whether a work is copyrighted. If the book does turn out to be in the public domain, you could rewrite these historical accounts, bringing the language up-to-date and then send queries to publishers particularly interested in American history, as listed in *Writer's Market.*

Performance is Not "Publication"

Q. It is possible that I will give oral nonprofit readings of poetry that is under contract for future book publication. Would such readings in any way endanger my present common law copyright or my future statutory copyright? Is there any good practical reason to first copyright such poetry as a lecture, and then later change its category to a book?

A. Your common law copyright should serve to protect your poetry in your oral readings of it. Under the present copyright law, a poem can be performed while retaining its common law protection; the term of statutory copyright won't begin until that work achieves *printed* publication.

Poetry Book

Q. In arranging to publish a volume of one's poems, what is the proper and simplest procedure for securing release of copyright from publishers of magazines where the poems first appeared? (1) Must individual letters be written to each editor giving the titles and dates of publication of the various verses or (2) Could one make up a mimeo-

graphed form in sets of three and a very simple request note? Supposing a magazine has now ceased publication and possibly the original publisher or editor is deceased. Could one just ignore a release request?

A. The basic letter can be the same; all you'd have to do would be to change the poem titles and publication dates for each. So a mimeographed form would probably save you some time. Even though the magazine is no longer being published or the copyright owner is deceased, the copyright still continues to run the course of its 28-year term and would be owned either by the publisher or his heirs. The release request should *not* be ignored. You may have to write to the United States Copyright Office for the most recent address on its records for the copyright owner.

Fictional Dialogue in a Biography?

Q. In the writing of biographies for children, is it possible to make the reading more interesting by the use of fictional dialogue and setting? If so, what are the extents of the liberties which must be taken in order to assure a relatively accurate account of the nonfictional material while providing "readability" for youngsters?

A. Fictionalized biographies are frequently used for both adult and juvenile readers. Working with the basic facts, you may create conversations and incidents that will best dramatize them. But be careful not to devise anything that would not be in keeping with the character of the subject or his times.

Children's Plays

Q. My problem concerns a children's play I have written in which some of the characters are dolls and cartoon characters which have been made into dolls (Popeye, Bugs Bunny, Chatty Cathy, etc.). Do I have to obtain permission from these doll manufacturers and the cartoon originators before I can use them? If so, how? I would also appreciate any information you might give me concerning markets for children's plays.

A. When in doubt it is always safest to ask for permission. Write to the doll manufacturers (any large toy shop could provide their names and addresses) and to the cartoon originators in care of the movie studios or newspapers that present their work. Explain your project and request permission to use the characters' names in the way you have described. Be sure to enclose a stamped, self-addressed envelope. Some of the markets for children's plays are: *The Dramatic Publishing Co.* (86 E. Randolph St., Chicago, Ill. 60601); *Plays,* The Drama Magazine for Young People (8 Arlington Street, Boston, Mass. 02116); Instructor Publications, Dansville, N.Y. 11437, publishers of *The Instructor.*

Copyright Reference

Q. I would appreciate it if you could refer me to a good simplified reference book pertaining to copyright laws concerning use of reference material for article writing.

A. See a copy of *A Copyright Guide,* by Harriet F. Pilpel and Morton David Goldberg, published by R. R. Bowker Co. in cooperation with The Copyright Society of the U.S.A., New York, 1963.

Permission to Quote

Q. If I want to include a remark (good or bad) in an article of mine, about a magazine or article I have read, or comment on something I saw on TV, am I free to do so or do I have to have permission of the writer? I'm not going to quote, but will mention actual names.

A. You may make whatever comments you wish concerning actual names and places without getting permission of the people involved. Just make sure your statements are accurate.

Will the Real JB Stand Up?

Q. How careful must a fiction writer be with names he contrives but which could very well turn out to be the names of living persons? For example, I name the villain in a story Jack Bowlton. Could a real Jack Bowlton pop up and sue me for defamation of character for characterizing him as a villain? Also, what became of the old disclaimer which used to read something like "Any similarity to persons, etc., is strictly coincidental"?

A. Unless the real Jack Bowlton happened to circumstantially be very similar in personality and in actions to the fictional character you gave that name,

I don't see how there would be any cause for legal recourse. The old disclaimer probably doesn't appear any more because the person who can prove that a real person was used in a fictional account and can prove defamation or invasion of privacy may still have legal recourse in spite of the disclaimer.

Religious Order

Q. I am preparing to write a novel with a religious order as the background. All of the characters are fictional but I would like to use fact for places, rules of the order and other pertinent data. Is it necessary to get permission from the Superiors of this order?

A. I think to gain the specific practical information you need, yes, it would be best to contact the Superiors of the order about which you will be writing in your novel.

Old Songs

Q. I have read children's plays in which poems were sung to the tunes of old-fashioned songs. Where do the authors write to get permission to use such old airs as "Flow Gently Sweet Afton," "Jingle Bells", etc.?

A. Anyone may use such music without getting permission because these songs are in the public domain. Well-known songs and their copyright dates are indexed by title in the *Variety Music Cavalcade* available in large public libraries.

Reprint Rights?

Q. As a newcomer to the writing profession, I find the procedure for reselling an article or story confusing. Having used the *Writer's Market* as a guide, I find many publishers listed as buying first and second rights. Is this publisher purchasing the right to print an article twice, or do the terms mean he will consider material in which the author retains one right or the other? After a story has been sold once, does the term 'second rights' apply to each consecutive sale or do third and fourth rights apply or do reprint rights come into effect? Also, if a publisher has a policy of purchasing first serial rights, must the author request, in writing, reprint rights, or is this simply a matter of courtesy? Much of my writing has been to small religious magazines. I have been told that the possibilities of selling a story numerous times are good because of non-conflicting circulation. Supposing a story has already sold three times. Would I signify this by printing 'Reprint Rights' (or whatever is the correct term) in the right hand corner, followed by the names of the three publishing companies and the dates purchased, or is this listing unnecessary?

A. When a publisher buys first and second rights it means he will consider material which either has not been published before or which has been previously published. Second rights means he buys (usually for a lower price) the right to publish again an article or story or poem which has already appeared in another non-competing publication.

Yes, if a publisher purchases first serial rights, the author must request permission from the original publisher for transfer of other rights back to him. Yes it would be good to type in the upper right hand corner of your manuscript "reprint rights offered" and then perhaps as a last page to the manuscript list the places the story has previously appeared or been purchased.

Watch the Check Too!

Q. If I sell a novellette (long story) to any publisher, and some movie producer reads it in the publisher's magazine and wants to buy the movie rights, does he buy from me or the publisher? Must I reserve some kind of rights? Would the publisher be entitled to part of the money paid for the movie rights?

A. Reserving the movie rights to a novellette, depends on what rights you sell to the magazine in which it initially appears. Most magazines buy only "first serial rights" (for publication in a newspaper or magazine). Some magazines, however, buy "all rights" which would give them the complete return of money on any subsidiary sale of the story to the movies, television, etc. If you want to reserve these other rights to yourself, then when you submit your novellette to a magazine publisher, type in the upper right hand corner "First North American Serial Rights Only."

That will then indicate to the magazine that these are the only rights you care to sell to the story at that time. You should, however, also notice any check you receive from a magazine publisher since sometimes the endorsements on the check indicate that the magazine is buying all rights. Often the Accounting Department of a magazine does not know what your manuscript indicated and if their normal procedure would be to buy all rights the check will so indicate. By signing the check, you would be thereby giving away the rest of the rights, even though your manuscript had indicated you were only interested in selling first rights.

Resell?

Q. I do not understand the system of "rights." Does this mean that if I sell a story to one magazine that I could resell the same story to another magazine?

A. Many different rights (serial, book, TV, etc.), are involved in a literary property. If you sold only "first serial rights," for example, you could resell a story that had previously appeared in another magazine.

Recipe Book

Q. I have an idea for a specialized cook book. Is it permissible to use recipes from other books which are of this specialty or must all the recipes be my own original concoctions?

A. If the published recipes are under copyright and you intend to copy them word-for-word and/or ingredient-for-ingredient, then you will need to secure permission from the copyright owner.

Stole Your Story?

Q. In a recent issue of a magazine appeared an article on the medical profession that was strikingly similar to an essay I had written three years before, even to the title. The general content of the essay was the appalling lack of sympathy on the part of doctors today, even down to specific allusions, similes and general wording. I know that my essay was seen by several people in the "literary" world, and I'm naturally suspicious. However, I am really upset to think that I am forced to forget about submitting my piece anywhere else as they are so similar.

A. It is one of the frustrating facts of the freelance writer's life to find that an idea he has, someone else has also had and has beaten him to publication with it—sometimes even using the same words. You're not forced to forget about submitting your manuscript elsewhere. Many articles are published on the same subject in a variety of publications within a two or three year period. If your article is well written, and hits the right magazine at the right time, publication of this other article will not

Who Owns What?

Q. I should like to put my question in the form of a hypothetical case: Suppose Smith wrote a manuscript, in first draft, and gave it to Jones to read. Jones, a professional writer, keeps the manuscript, and in due time writes a book based on Smith's manuscript. If the book sells, and/or a movie is made

from it, and/or paperbacks are published, or any other form of benefit derives from the sale of this book, does Smith have any rights in this book or the benefits therefrom?

A. Much would depend on whatever agreement Smith made with Jones when he gave him his manuscript. Why, for instance, did Smith allow Jones to keep the manuscript? However, Smith might be able to take this matter to court as the infringement of his common law copyright which protected his unpublished manuscript. In doing so, though, he'd have to prove that Jones actually copied his exact language or the development, treatment, arrangement or sequence of ideas in the work. And he would have to take legal action within the period of the applicable Statute of Limitations. It would, of course, be more desirable if Smith and Jones could work out some financial arrangement agreeable to both, rather than go to the expense of court action.

Translation Rights

Q. A few months ago, while in Vienna, I read in an Austrian magazine a short article which I found impressive. I asked the doctor-author for the translation rights into English which he gladly gave me. Under whose name should one ask for the copyright, in the name of the author or that of the translator?

A. Publishers of periodicals usually copyright all articles, and then, upon request, will often assign the copyright to the author. In the case of a translation, the assignment of copyright will depend on the deal made between the owner of the basic copyright and the translator. You will have to settle this question with the doctor who granted you the translation rights. (Incidentally, you had best also make sure the doctor *had* the rights to give you. Query the Austrian magazine to verify that he had the translation rights.)

A. You will have to check with the publisher who purchased your confession stories to determine who owns the copyright, book rights, etc. You will not be able to register the rewritten stories with the Copyright Office because they are already protected by common law copyright in *unpublished* form. To obtain a copyright on them in book form, the book must be published and carry the copyright notice.

Book Rights to Stories

Q. Does a writer retain subsequent rights to his own stories published in a magazine? I have had seven confession stories purchased and printed by one company. Now I want to market these pieces as a collection in one book-form manuscript. Do I need permission from the original publisher? Suppose I rewrite these stories and have them registered as a book manuscript with the Copyright Office in Washington— would I then be able to offer it for sale?

Chapter 32

Short Story Writing

Adult Fiction?

Q. Could you please define exactly what adult fiction is?

A. Adult fiction simply means that the characters, their problems and experiences, and the style of writing are intended for grownup readers rather than children and teenagers.

Story Titles

Q. In submitting short fiction to general slick magazines, what is the best procedure to follow when a good title does not come to mind? Is it better to submit an untitled story or to submit a title that does not satisfy the author? In these circumstances, should a letter accompany the piece explaining that a title is lacking and the author would like the story titled by the magazine, or that the author feels the title submitted is unsatisfactory? Also, what is the procedure to follow in submitting to confession magazines? If a title is submitted, should it follow the pattern used in the magazines?

A. Titles are often subject to change by the magazines; therefore don't spend too much time worrying about them. For purposes of identification, it *is* advisable for a manuscript to have a title, so choose a simple one rather than none at all. Do not enclose any explanatory letters.

Definitions, Please

Q. Many magazines' fiction requirements specify either "no contrived" or "no slick" stories. So far as I can determine, "contrived," means planned (what story isn't planned?) and "slick" means on slick paper (many types of stories are on slick paper). Could you please give me your definition of these terms?

A. By "contrived," these magazines usually mean plots whose action is constructed in an artificial, implausible way. For example, if a character purposely sets fire to a barn to kill the man inside, that's a credible, well-motivated act. But if a fire happens to break out in the barn for no reason other than the obvious one of helping the author dispose of the man inside, that's contrived. "Slick" *did* originally refer only to the type of paper used in a magazine. But nowadays, it has come to mean the familiar, formula-type story, e.g., boy meets girl—loses girl—gets girl, which has a neat, pat (and usually happy) ending.

Problem With Heirs?

Q. I know of no living relatives belonging to the real-life character I am basing my short story on. Am I free to continue my short fiction without thought of his living heirs?

A. Go ahead and write your story, being careful not to falsify the facts, damage the man's reputation or in any way malign him. In short, write nothing that could conceivably make you the victim of a lawsuit, should any of his heirs be extant.

Children's Stories

Q. I would like to specialize in writing for children but I need some basic instruction in how to go about this. What do you suggest?

A. *Writing for Children and Teenagers* by Lee Wyndham is a good basic reference in this field. You'll find detailed chapters on how to get ideas, how to handle characterization, dialogue, plotting, motivation, conflict, suspense— and then how to sell it after you write it.

Rule Breakers

Q. Maugham and Hemingway were both considered great writers. But most of their short stories did not have plots, that is "conflict." If either writer were alive today, would their stuff sell?

A. Works that have become classics have the ability to go beyond the narrow time in which they were produced because of the universal truths and insights they offer. The stories of these writers do sell today because of their author's inherent skill in bringing characters to life and making their problems interesting. Their work does indeed deal with the conflicts of man's relation to man and to himself.

Settings are Scenes

Q. How does one go about isolating a scene, in dissecting a short story? To me the scenes seem somewhat continuous. I fail to see any sharp dividing line in a taut story.

A. Whenever the action moves to a different setting, that's automatically a new scene. If, for example, a story opens in a young couple's kitchen and then moves to an incident in the husband's office, these two different settings constitute two different scenes. But suppose the story is a taut short-short in which all the action takes place in the kitchen. Then we look for a division that is not geographical but a time change. This could develop if your first scene shows the husband and wife in the kitchen at breakfast time. Then after setting this stage, you may want to have a time break to five o'clock when the wife is preparing dinner. This is a device used often. For example, "Jim stomped out during breakfast without finishing his coffee. As Ellen prepared dinner, she thought of the silly argument they had had early that day."

Fiction Query?

Q. What should the fiction writer put in his query? Should the smaller, less well-known publications be queried at all? What should be the length?

A. Because of the nature of fiction, editors rarely if ever expect to be queried about it. Good fiction usually defies the type of summarization or highlighting used in query letters because so many of the integral elements, e.g. style, mood, characterization, etc., would be lost. Therefore, to consider fiction fairly, most editors prefer to receive the manuscript in toto.

One Part to Two Part?

Q. After I have sold a short-short story, can I take the story and expand it into a two or three-part story and sell it again?

A. The answer to this would depend on what rights you offered for sale along with your story. If the magazine you sold your story to bought only the usual First North American Serial Rights, then this means that after its appearance in this magazine just this one time, all rights to the story reverted to you.

You would then be free to do what you wished with it. Simply write a letter to the purchaser of your story, asking about the rights involved in this transaction. It would be ethical to tell whomever you're going to sell subsequent versions of the story to, of the story's original sales record.

Famous Name?

Q. At what time is it permissible to use the name of a famous person in a short story? If the name was not used in an unfavorable manner, would there be any objections?

A. Provided there are no derogatory connotations, it is permissible to use a famous person's name in a short story.

Non-Formula Story

Q. How do I write the story that is not the "formula" story? ... Every story has its beginning, middle and its ending. When studying a story an editor has called the "no formula" story, I cannot see any difference from that which is called the "formula" story ... except for the opening of that story. Setting the scene is generally used as the opening for any good story, but a story that is not considered "formula" seems to open without the setting of a scene or background. Is this the only difference or have I failed to receive the message?

A. The message you're getting is a little garbled. While the opening of a story sometimes is a clue as to whether or not it is a "formula" story, *that* is not one of the significant differences between "formula" and "non-formula" fiction. When editors speak of the formula story, they usually mean a familiar theme treated in a predictable or familiar plot structure. Thus, the formula for the slick love story might be: boy meets girl, boy loses girl, boy gets girl. The editor who is looking for a non-formula story wants to get away from such plot situations and development. He wants an unusual central problem treated in an original manner. Very likely the character in the story will be more responsible for carrying the plot along than the situation. The stories in *Esquire* frequently provide examples of the non-formula type.

Young Author

Q. I have a boxful of short stories, ranging in length from 8 to 110 handwritten pages. Since I'm only 14, I wonder if there's any market you could suggest for my work or am I too young? Too, must all submitted manuscripts be typed? I find it most impossible to sit down at a typewriter and express myself.

A. You are never too young to submit your work to markets, provided it is salable. But before you do, I would advise you to read and become thoroughly familiar with the magazines you're interested in writing for. There are many young people's publications, and you'll find a list of them in the *Writer's Market*. Try to decide what age group would be most interested in your stories and then study any large newsstand to learn about the magazines that are geared to this readership group. It is recommended that manuscripts be typed. However, there's no reason why you can't initially "express yourself" in longhand and then type up the manuscript for submission to markets.

Short Story Prize

Q. I am writing a novel and I need to know in connection with the plot, what are the well known prizes for short stories, similar, say, to the Pulitzer prize or Nobel prize.

A. There are no prizes for individual short stories comparable to the Nobel for the novel. A Pulitzer Prize in fiction might be given for a collection of short stories by a single author. Other awards given to short stories are those which are included each year in the two volumes of *Best Short Stories of the Year*. One of these is called the O'Henry Awards and this annual volume was published by Doubleday and Company in 1968. The other book is called *The Best Short Stories of 1968*, etc. It is edited by Martha Foley and David Burnett and the book was published last year by the Houghton Mifflin Company.

Fact Into Fiction

Q. What rules pertain to fictionalizing an actual event about which there was considerable mystery and secrecy? The event was a semi-scientific experiment which was unique and which received nation-wide publicity when it occurred. Since the event was unique and widely publicized, the event and all of its participants would be easily recognized. Because military security is still in effect about the experiment, I am sure there is no possibility of doing a factual piece on the subject. Where and how is the line drawn between fact and fiction in such a case? To what degree would the event and characters have to be changed to make them fictitious?

A. Since the event received such widespread publicity, you may use a similar idea in a fiction plot, but you would be wise to surround it with a new, invented set of characters (e.g., one character could be made considerably younger than the real-life one, and given different personal traits and appearance), and sufficiently altered circumstances (perhaps in a different locale) so that the resultant story will be the product of your own creativity rather than just straight reporting.

More True-Life Problems

Q. My short story embraces a particular true event in a nineteenth century man's life which is recorded in newspapers and books. Can I properly call it fiction even though two-thirds of the story is my own dialogue and events? I wish to be fair.

A. Yes, it is certainly permissible to fictionalize an historical event. Since you are creating the dialogue and much of the dramatic action, it can properly be called fiction.

Use Real Names?

Q. In a juvenile fiction story based on true historical incidents, may I use authentic names of teachers, mayors, ministers, business men etc.?

A. If there is nothing derogatory in your references to these people, there should be no objection to your use of their names.

Chapter 33

Song Titles and Lyrics

Songwriting

Q. I feel that I have a talent for song writing, and have composed many songs in my spare time, just for the fun of it. Now, I would like to get serious about it. How can I inexpensively protect my material until I find out if it's any good?

A. The only way to protect your songs is to copyright them—since this is one of the few forms of an unpublished manuscript which can be copyrighted. The price is $6.00 per song and you can write for application blanks to the Registrar of Copyrights, Library of Congress, Washington, D.C.

Music Markets?

Q. Where can I get a list of music markets? I write a great deal of music, and you used to list such markets.

A. We had to discontinue carrying the list of music publishers in the *Writer's Market* because the song business, as you know, has changed so radically in the last few years. Most songs today have to be sold in person to record company representatives rather than to music publishers. It's very hard to deal with this market by mail.

Copyrighting Songs

Q. Does the Library of Congress Circular #22 cover only books, or songs also?

A. Circular #22 deals mainly with Searches for Copyright and covers musical works as well as books. There is also Circular #67 that concerns the copyright registration of poems and song lyrics.

Song Title Protection

Q. I have several proposed titles to songs that ought to be popular, and suggested lyrics for them, but I fear if they were sent to song-writing people, I'd have no protection. If I'd get a song copyrighted, the title could be snatched, couldn't it?

A. Titles as such are not subject to copyright. However, it is possible to get the lyrics copyrighted. There is a free circular, #67, entitled "Poems and Song Lyrics" which you may obtain by writing to the Copyright Office, Library of Congress, Washington, D.C., 20540. This will tell you what can be copyrighted in this field and which forms to request.

Chapter 34

What Is Style?

Personal Style

Q. I recently read an article by a well known fiction writer who said it was not good to read other fiction writers. He stated it would confuse his style and it may make his work seem inferior to the other writers. What is the majority's opinion on this matter?

A. The narrow view of that particular writer is not generally shared by most writers who have one love in common— the love of reading. If reading the work of others confuses a writer's style, then such a style was probably not individual enough or rooted deeply enough to begin with. The novice writer may go through several phases of stylistic expression before he finds the one that is himself. Remember that a writer who reads only himself may find that he is writing only for himself too.

A Question on Style

Q. I am puzzled by the idea of style. Also I would appreciate a list of the various types of style, so that I can make a study of them.

A. Every writer has his own style because style is simply the way in which an author expresses his ideas. Faulkner's style, for example, is recognizably different from Hemingway's. It would be impossible to list all the various styles because of the diversity of the individuals producing them. The best way to study authors' styles is to read their works. For additional help in improving your own style, see *Elements of Style* by Strunk & White.

First Person Always True?

Q. How can a humorous book written in the first person (such as those by Jean Kerr) be thought of as fiction, even allowing for exaggerated anecdotes?

A. While probably inspired by factual bits and pieces in the writer's life, essentially these books are more imagination than reality. Writing in the first person doesn't necessarily guarantee that the material is true.

Chapter 35

Submitting Your Manuscripts

Fold or Flat?

Q. I have read that manuscripts under 12 pages may be mailed folded in thirds. Is this true?
A. It is customary to fold only manuscripts that are under 5 pages. Anything over this should be mailed flat.

Cover Letter?

Q. I have submitted many things to various publishers in the juvenile field and I find it more difficult to write the "cover letter" than the manuscript itself. To date I have not had anything published except newspaper articles so do not include any "credits" in my cover letter. I understand it should be short—but how short?
A. It's not even necessary to submit a cover letter with a manuscript. If your article or story is completely written in the proper form, it can just be submitted with a self-addressed stamped envelope and no cover letter. If you do wish to include a cover letter anyway, all it would have to say would be "Dear Editor: Here's an article (or short story) that I think might be of interest to your readers because (and then tell why). May I have a report from you on it within 30 days? Thank you."

To Glue or Not?

Q. In an earlier issue of WD the fiction editor of *Good Housekeeping* was quoted as pleading with writers to affix, rather than attach, return postage on the return envelope. Yet, I've had official professional instruction to attach it. What to do?
A. This is one case where editors usually prefer to take a licking! Some editors feel it saves valuable time in their offices. There is also less danger of losing the stamps when they're pasted onto the return envelope.

Resubmitting Mss.

Q. One of my stories was published in an amateur magazine (I received no money). May I send it now to another magazine for money?

146

A. Yes, but there are several things to keep in mind. First, if the magazine was not copyrighted, your material is now in the public domain and anyone could have re-used it as is. To submit it now to a magazine and get it copyrighted, as part of the magazine, it would have to be revised sufficiently to be considered a "new work" by the Copyright Office. If the magazine in which it originally appeared *was* copyrighted, you'd have to clear with the editor whether they bought only first rights or "all rights" to the material.

Poetry Book

Q. I am submitting a volume of poetry for consideration in a contest open to those who have not yet published a complete volume. What procedures should be followed about the inclusion of poetry previously published (and most of them are)? Does it suffice to list the magazines in which they appeared or must permission be sought for each poem specifically?

A. If this contest involves the eventual publishing of the winning poetry books and if your poems originally appeared in copyrighted publications, you should secure permission. Acknowledgement of such permission can be made in a prefatory statement.

Mailing Carton

Q. Can you give me the address of a supplier of carton containers for the purpose of mailing book manuscripts?

A. Yes, among the suppliers of carton containers for mailing book manuscripts, one is Logan Enterprises, Dept. WD., P.O. Box 7368, St. Petersburg, FL 33734

Tear Sheets

Q. In free-lancing, it is often necessary to submit a tear sheet or sample of some previously published work. How are these usually obtained?

A. Publishers frequently furnish free tear sheets on request. If these are not available, you may offer to buy copies of the issue either from the publisher or from back-issue magazine dealers. Photo copies may be made on machines in most large libraries, but these are not as desirable as actual sample pages.

Multiple Editor?

Q. When submitting to an editor who edits one or more related magazines, should one submit to each magazine separately or to the editor? Also, I recently sold a story to a Sunday School paper to which I do not have access. Would it be proper to write them to send me copies when it is published?

A. Send your manuscript to the editor in care of whichever magazine is your first choice. If he finds it more suited to another of his magazines, he will consider it accordingly. It *is* permissible to write the publisher, tactfully requesting the publication date and a copy of the issue in which your story appears. Many publishers automatically send out complimentary copies upon publication.

How to Submit Poetry

Q. Must poetry always be double-spaced? Length requirements are given in numbers of lines. Does number of lines, then, replace the usual word count? Or should both be given? How does one arrange the manuscript for a book of verse? One poem to a page? Or in that order which the author feels would appear to best advantage in the printed work? If illustrations are offered, how should the page for which they are intended be indicated? What are the established minimum or maximum length requirements for the book of verse? Is it wise to combine humorous and inspirational verse in a single volume?

A. Longer poetry, usually more than three stanzas, may be single-spaced. It is not necessary to include a word count, only a line count. Prepare the manuscript with one poem to a page, in the order you prefer. And insert the illustrations, also one to a page, where you would like them in the printed version. In view of your two different themes, it might be helpful to divide the volume into two sections, with appropriate headings for both the inspirational and the humorous segments. There are no strict rules about length, but it would be a good idea to have at least twenty poems.

Return Postage on Books?

Q. Should return postage be enclosed with book-length manuscripts? I've never done this, and manuscripts have been returned without any request for postage.

A. You have been fortunate to encounter publishers kind enough to assume this cost! Actually, sufficient return postage should definitely be clipped to the letter you enclose or to the first page of your manuscript.

Picture Book Ms

Q. I recently submitted a manuscript of a child's picture book to a book critic. He said it was excellent and could make no suggestions for improvement, and that in its "final" form, it should sell. I had the story typed the same as a fiction manuscript. Is there a special form for picture books?

A. Picture book manuscripts are often submitted with only one or two sentences per page, the way they might appear when accompanied by illustrations in the printed book. To be on the safe side, why don't you ask that book critic what *he* meant by "final form"?

Male Confession Writer?

Q. Does a male writer, writing as a female, have a chance in the confession markets? Is it true that some of these publications require an affidavit attesting to the truth of the story?

A. Since confessions do not carry by-lines, men have just as good a chance as women in this field, provided they can write convincingly from a female viewpoint. If a confession seems "true" to readers, that's all that counts; affidavits aren't necessary.

Christmas Ideas

Q. I always have such good Christmas ideas when the Christmas issues come out. When should these ideas be sent in and to whom should they be sent?

A. Submit your Christmas ideas to the Nonfiction Editor at least 6-8 months in advance of the season.

Do Credits Help?

Q. I have finally made a short story sale. Should I indicate that on the first page of my mss to insure more careful consideration?

A. Since most editors prefer to judge a fiction manuscript solely on its own merit, it is better not to try to impress them with a list of credits. A record of past sales won't increase the chances of a good story or make a poor one sound any better.

Counting Words

Q. How do I count the number of words in a mss and must it be sent flat or can it be folded?

A. Every word counts. The word "a" counts as a word. Abbreviated words count as one word. Count the exact number of words on three representative pages, and from the average number of words per page compute the number of words in the manuscript. In a longer script, of say fifty pages, you should count exactly the number of words on five pages and compute the total from that. Manuscripts under five pages can be folded in thirds but longer manuscripts should be sent flat.

Missing Mss

Q. What does a writer do if his manuscript never comes back? Can I make a duplicate copy and send it to another publisher?

A. Inform the magazine to which you've sent your manuscript that you are officially withdrawing it from their consideration. You may then send your story elsewhere, but be sure you type up a fresh new original and hang on to the carbon copy of both your letter and the new ms.

Free Contributions

Q. Would editors of publications accept free contributions from the authors? Or would this be infringing on some free-lance writer who has to be paid in order to live? My reason for asking this is because I would like to see some of my material published, material for which I do not feel I should accept money to have it get to the public. It is moralistic writing and does carry a message. What say you?

A. There are some magazines that do not offer any payment for contributions. However, if it is the magazine's policy to pay for the material they use, then you should not offer them your contribution free. Do not be misled into thinking that just because it's free, an editor will use it. If, in the editor's estimation, it's worthy of being printed, he will gladly pay for it (and you can send the check to your favorite charity). If it doesn't seem publishable to him, then the fact that it's free will not persuade him that it should be used anyway.

Then too, this giving away of material is unfair competition to writers who *do* need the money (and most writers *do!*). So go along with the policy of the magazine. If there are no takers ... and you're burning to get this message into print(and money is no object), you can always reach the public by buying advertising space.

Multiple Query?

Q. Is it permissible to submit a query covering the same article to two different editors at the same time? Sometimes the time element is important and if one editor delays answering, it could be too late to query another.

A. It is permissible, but not always practical, to submit the same article idea to several magazines simultaneously. Most writers abhor the long delay it takes to get an answer from a magazine editor, but realize on the other hand, that if they do make simultaneous submissions to editors they are going to face the possible situation of more than one editor asking to see the article and having to be told that someone else is considering it and they would have to wait. Naturally an editor who is told that he will have to wait in line, is not going to look very kindly on the next letter from that particular writer. In the case of article ideas which are timely, many freelance writers use this technique: they point out in the letter to the editor that it is an extremely timely query and they would request a reply in so many days. Most editors would respect this request.

Submitting a Book

Q. What are the special angles a writer should watch in submitting his finished book length ms to a publisher?

A. Keep a carbon: If your manuscript is lost, regardless of whether you sent it registered mail, the publisher will not bear the cost of retyping. Therefore, always retain a carbon. Do *not* bind or staple a ms. Enclose return postage. Type your name and address on the title page and your name only on each succeeding page in the upper left-hand corner. What you have to say belongs in the book. Any matter enclosed in a covering letter that is not specifically important cannot help you, and might hurt. In a covering letter belongs a list of your previously published works only if of some importance, and issued by a respected publisher, as well as information regarding documentary evidence to support any facts in the book that might be questioned.

Quoting Copyrighted Material

Q. I wish to quote a couple of paragraphs of copyrighted material in a novel. Am I required to obtain permission to quote before submitting the ms or is this the responsibility of the publisher who accepts the work?

A. When submitting your novel manuscript to a publisher, you should include a page indicating the source of the original copyrighted material you used, so he can request permission to use it if it remains in the final version of the novel he accepts for publication.

Mailing Query Letters

Q. What do you suggest for mailing queries: in a ten-inch envelope with a six-incher for the return or in an eleven-inch envelope with a ten-incher for the return?

A. The eleven-inch envelope with a ten-incher return would probably have a neater appearance, especially since the editor may return your query letter along with his answer.

Fillers

Q. What are the rules on submitting identical fillers to the 150-200 word $1.00-$2.50 markets?

A. It is usually ethical to submit a filler to only one market at a time.

Foreign Market

Q. What procedure does one follow for submitting manuscripts to publishers abroad? The difficulty seems to be in getting them back again at a reasonable rate of postage. Is there any cheaper method than the International Postal Exchange Coupon which I understand is limited to first class?

A. The International Postal Exchange Coupon is the most convenient method of handling the return postage. However, to save wear and tear on the book-length manuscript, simply send a brief synopsis, some sample chapters (consecutive ones if possible) and a query letter. In this way, the postage there and back would be less expensive too.

Simultaneous Submission

Q. A playwright I know sends out seven copies of his plays at once to various producers. He claims it is all right to do the same with fiction and non-fiction, and the first editor that offers to buy, then you can just sell. If two editors make offers, then you can take the best offer, or even bargain. Is it all right to do this without telling the editor it is a simultaneous submission?

A. Your friend is playing with fire. Unless a magazine is known to accept simultaneous submissions, (and there are some, in the religious field—see *Writer's Market*); it would be best to submit fiction or non-fiction to just one editor at a time. Many editors just won't read a manuscript that they know another editor is considering. And if they *don't* know it and happen to be the loser in a two-editor interest in a ms, they're not likely ever to read *another* ms submitted by that writer.

Withdraw Manuscript?

Q. If a magazine refuses to return a story or article after many months, refuses to reply to inquiries, is it proper (legal?) to send a registered letter informing the editor that as of a certain date you intend to submit the material to other publications? Or are you at the mercy of the guilty magazine?

A. Yes, the right thing to do is to send a registered letter informing the editor that as of a certain date, you intend to submit your material to other publications.

Double Submissions

Q. Is it a good or bad practice to submit more than one short-story manuscript to an editor at one time?

A. Though it means more waiting, it is advisable to submit only one short-story manuscript at a time. If the first is accepted, the editor will be happy to receive another one from you at a later date. If the first is rejected, its weaknesses, fresh in the editor's mind, may inadvertently minimize the merits of the second which is read immediately after the first.

Submitting a Book

Q. In your August, 1967 issue I found the article "How to avoid the book publisher's slush pile" most interesting and informative. However, I am a bit puzzled. The author, Peter S. Prescott, noted (in how to submit a manuscript) that such a manuscript should be put in a box—not a home-sewn binding or a clip-board spring cover. Does this mean that the manuscript should be submitted with individual *loose* pages? Secondly, is it preferable to submit the original copy of the manuscript, or will a carbon copy run the gauntlet just as well?

A. Yes, the individual pages should be loose in the box in which you are submitting a book manuscript. Editors prefer this to having to hold a bulky, bound manuscript to read. Yes, it is preferable to submit the original copy and many publishers will not even read a carbon copy.

Mailing Book Mss

Q. Please let us know what you think of sending book-length manuscripts in "jiffy bags," and enclosing correct return postage.

A. It's a "novel" idea, but a cardboard box is still the safest way to pack such manuscripts to prevent corners from bending, etc.

Selling Plays

Q. I am in need of information concerning requirements for play submission; whether sales are made on a cash or royalty basis; information concerning rights, and a list of reputable agents. Also needed is information on the Dramatists Guild contract that says the author can demand his living expense away from home or on tour for participating in production. I wish to know whether this pertains to previously unproduced authors or just to members of the Guild.

A. Plays for the legitimate theater are handled through a dramatic agent and a list of these appears in our annual directory, *The Writer's Market*. Payments are made on a royalty basis usually with an advance payment to the author before the play opens. Complete details on the Dramatists Guild and their workings can be obtained from them and the address is 234 West 44th Street, New York, New York 10036. Plays are copyrighted by sending two copies of the play and six dollars to the Register of Copyrights, Library of Congress, Washington, D.C.

Submitting Play Mss

Q. Do all plays, one-act or full-length plays, have to be bound regardless of whether they are sent to a play publisher or to a producer or to a little theater? Some contest rules I received stated they would read only "bound" plays.

A. The request for "bound" plays is the exception rather than the rule. Play manuscripts being offered for sale are usually submitted *unbound,* free of staples or fasteners of any kind. Just make sure all your pages are clearly numbered and carry your last name.

Reprint Submissions

Q. How do I indicate on my manuscript that my articles have been previously published?

A. In the upper right hand corner of your first page, indicate "Second Rights" as well as the name and date of the publication in which this material first appeared.

Multiple Consideration

Q. How does one submit a manuscript to a firm when one wishes to have it considered for all their publications?

A. Send the manuscript directly to the publisher instead of to the individual magazines. The publisher's name and address can usually be found next to the copyright notice at the beginning of the magazine. The editors can then decide which, if any, of their publications your manuscript is best suited for.

Gag Submissions

Q. What is the standard way to submit gags to cartoonists?

A. On a 3x5 card or paper slip, neatly type a description of the scene and caption. You should stamp your name and address either on the front or back of this slip, and also specify a code number in an upper corner. This number plus your initials would be placed on the back of the cartoonist's rough, and used to identify the gagwriter. Mail the gag slip (keeping a carbon copy for yourself) in a 3½x6½ envelope and include a folded return envelope of the same size.

How Much Personal Background?

Q. I'm a beginning writer, but I don't think I have to scream the fact to an editor. How much information is it necessary to include with a manuscript? Also, what do editors think of short manuscripts sent folded in half in 6½ x9½ envelopes?

A. The only personal information necessary is your name and address in the upper lefthand corner of your manuscript. The manuscript folded in half in a 6½x9½ envelope is satisfactory, but be sure to enclose a stamped, self-addressed envelope too for the manuscript's safe return if it is not accepted.

Illustrations for Books

Q. What is the standard format for preparing illustrations for juvenile books? Also, is material considered more salable to juvenile publishers if accompanied by illustrations?

A. Publishers of juvenile books prefer manuscripts not to be accompanied by illustrations since they prefer to work directly with free-lance artists who know the publisher's mechanical requirements. There is no "standard format," though illustration board and opaque water colors are frequently used.

Canadian Writers

Q. Do Canadians stand an equal chance in the American market with people who live in the United States? Here, first class letter postage is five cents for the first ounce. I think your rate is six cents. How can one best manage return postage?

A. Yes, Canadians stand an equal chance in the American market, provided they are sending material that is competitive with what American writers can supply. Many Canadians solve the return postage problem by sending a check for the appropriate amount plus the Canadian exchange to the Postmaster of the nearest large American city requesting the Postmaster to send them an appropriate number of six cent American stamps.

Controversial Article

Q. Among several articles I hope to write is one of a very controversial nature. Even if an editor thinks the piece is interesting, he will likely want to be very sure of the authenticity of the source material—especially of an unknown writer. How do I proceed?

A. Most writers of controversial articles maintain a detailed list of their sources of information and have this ready for presentation to an editor who would question the author on any specific point. Send off your article or your article query and advise the editor you'll be glad to provide verification on any points he questions.

Series of Novels

Q. Is it proper to indicate in a cover letter that my novel is the first of a series? Also, should the publisher who accepted a portion of a series turn down any succeeding books in that series, would it be ethical to submit these to another publisher?

A. Indicate the proposed series, but do it in an initial query letter instead of submitting the completed manuscript. It is doubtful that the series could be divided among different publishers. But if you change the characters' names and make no references to events in previous books, there's no reason why these books couldn't be marketed on a separate basis lacking any tie-in with the series.

Booklength MS

Q. In mailing a book manuscript (often too large and unwieldly to be accommodated by even the largest manilas) how should one best prepare it to insure safe arrival? What provisions should be made for its return?

A. It is best to ship a bulky book manuscript in a neatly-wrapped corrugated box. It is customary to send manuscripts at the Special Fourth Class Book Rate of 12 cents for the first pound and 6 cents for each additional pound or fraction. Be sure to enclose return postage, and always keep carbon copies of all work sent out.

Submitting Greeting Card Verse

Q. What is meant by "identifying marks" on poems sent to greeting card firms?

A. Since such poems often do not have titles, it is a good idea to number them (one poem to a page), and keep carbon copies with the corresponding numbers for your own records. Then when paying for one from a group, the editor can refer to it by number.

Chapter 36

Editorial Taboos

Magazine Taboos

Q. What subjects are taboo in magazines?

A. Some magazines have no taboos, and state this in their editorial requirements in the *Writer's Market*. Others state what their particular taboos are. For instance you wouldn't submit an article about a plane wreck to an airlines magazine. Car magazines too sometimes specify no accidents. Many of the men's magazines use sexy stories; others are not markets for this type. The confession magazines are now accepting stories about racial and religious conflicts which were formerly taboo. Religious magazines have their special sets of taboos which vary from magazine to magazine. Church school papers use stories which follow the precepts of their particular religion. Some state flatly "No smoking, drinking, dancing, etc." When writing for the youngest of the juvenile set, keep the ending happy. You should also write for sample copies of the magazines you plan to submit to, and study them to see just what they use.

Teen-Age Smokers?

Q. I'm writing a book. Will I hurt my chances of publication if I have a few of my teenage characters smoking cigarettes? Can I name popular brands?

A. If smoking definitely contributes to your development of the characterizations in a realistic way, use it. It's all right to name popular brands provided no derogatory references are made to them.

Teen-Age Book

Q. If my story were acceptable in every other way, do you think that a publisher of teenage books would reject it because it has: 1) a fight between two teenage members of a high school football team; 2) a college-ager who is restricted to a wheelchair because of a football injury; 3) football action that gets rough, i.e. an elbow thrown at the face, nothing worse; 4) another character getting his arm broken in practice? I need to know if these could be objectionable or if there is some other flaw to my book which has met with rejections.

A. It is highly doubtful that any of these elements alone could be responsible for the rejection of your book manuscript. Other factors, such as style, plotting, credibility, etc., should be considered.

Chapter 37

Writing for Television

TV Scripts

Q. On completion of an hour-long TV script adapted for a program that is filmed in California, would it be wiser to contact an agent in New York or California or would it make any difference?

A. If the film producer is located in California, then it would be better to work with an agent who is in the same area.

Book To TV

Q. How can, or can a writer submit his book to a production studio for possible televising as a series; also does this apply to published stories in magazines? Can you market a manuscript if it is a story used as a series in another magazine?

A. Most television producers work through agents who know the markets available for various story themes, treatment, etc. This material may be in the form of a short story, a play or a book from which a script can be writ-

ten. If a story is used as a series in a magazine, then the author will have to check with the magazine publisher to determine who owns the TV rights. If the author owns them, he is free to negotiate with TV agents. A list of agents and indications of whether or not they will work with previously unproduced writers appears in the *Writer's Market*.

TV Script Length?

Q. Could you please tell me how many typewritten pages there are in the average half-hour TV script and the approximate number in an hour-long teleplay.

A. In general, there would be approximately 30 pages in the half-hour script and about 75 pages in the hour-long script.

TV "Treatment" and "Outline"

Q. What is the difference between "treatment" and "outline" specifically in reference to its use in the Nancy Vogel article on TV writing in March '64 *Writer's Digest?*

A. An outline is a short, concise synopsis of the story. The "treatment" is a scene-by-scene explanation, indicating the specific action, motivation, possible special effects, etc. It provides a fuller interpretation of the script's potential.

Script Protection

Q. I seek information about protecting manuscripts submitted to agents. In particular reference to television scripts.

A. Non-members of the Writers' Guild of America can mail their television scripts to that Guild with a check for $5.00 and have the script registered as to its completion date. The address of the Writers' Guild is 8955 Beverly Boulevard, Los Angeles, California 90048.

Chapter 38

Foreign Language Translations

Resell Foreign Story

Q. I speak and read French and found a marvelous short story in a foreign magazine I'd like to translate and sell to an American magazine. How do I do it?

A. If you have a facility with another language and would like to submit a translation of a foreign short story, you must write the publication in which the foreign short story appeared and get permission of both the author and the publisher to do your translation. Whether or not you would be required to share payment from the American publisher with either or both of the former depends on what arrangements you make with them. It's always wisest to clarify this point before you approach any American editor so there is no delay if he is interested in your idea.

Translation Markets

Q. What are the markets for translations of foreign stories, articles, books?

A. There are only a few specialized magazines such as the *American-* *Scandinavian Review* which have directly indicated their interest in translation material, but there's no reason not to try any magazine whose subject matter is similar to what you have to propose. (See procedure to follow in answer above.) A few book publishers have published translations of previously published foreign works. A way to find out who these books publishers are, is to look in the library at the *Subject Guide to Books in Print* under the category, for example, of "French—Translations From" and see which publishers are given. Other languages are similarly listed.

Translator Job

Q. How does one get a job as a translator? I speak German and English equally well and am also an aspiring writer. Could one start by translating technical articles or books? If so, how?

A. Translation jobs are available primarily with companies which have technical reports and correspondence to translate, although a few book publishers might be prospects. Rates for literary translations average about $15.00 per 1,000 words and are therefore less than scientific or industrial translation work which can bring up to $100.00 per 1,000 for specialized work. Some professional associations of translators which might be contacted for additional details on this subject include: American Translators Association, P. O. Box 489, Madison Square Station, New York, NY 10010 and Association of Professional Translators, Inc., 258 Broadway, R. 729, New York, NY 10007.

General Index